Praise for *Designing and Implementing Global Selection Systems*:

"Ryan and Tippins accurately capture the nuances, challenges and joys of instituting truly global selection tests and systems while providing practical advice and guidance. This book is a 'must read' for anyone with responsibility for global selection program

Karen B. Paul, Ph.D.,  *, 3M*

"Two master scientist-practiti account of best practices and selection system development. Blending theory and extensive concrete illustrations from applied work, this is a volume that no one with an interest in this topic should be without."

Paul Sackett, University of Minnesota

"This book provides well-written, practical, and user-friendly guidance for professionals who are working with selection systems in the global space. It is refreshing to have a book with a strong focus on the practical issues of designing and implementing quality selection systems for the global practitioner. This is an excellent primer for those new to selection as well as a good refresher for experienced practitioners."

Tanya Delany, PhD., IBM

Talent Management Essentials

Series Editor: Steven G. Rogelberg, Ph.D
Professor and Director Organizational Science, University of North Carolina – Charlotte

Senior Advisory Board:
- Eric Elder, Ph.D., Director, Talent Management, Corning Incorporated
- William H. Macey, Ph.D., Chief Executive Officer, Valtera Corporation
- Cindy McCauley, Ph.D., Senior Fellow, Center for Creative Leadership
- Elaine D. Pulakos, Ph.D., Chief Operating Officer, Personnel Decisions Research Institutes
- Douglas H. Reynolds, Ph.D., Vice President, Assessment Technology, Development Dimensions International
- Ann Marie Ryan, Ph.D., Professor, Michigan State University
- Lise Saari, Ph.D., Direct, Global Workforce Research, IBM
- John Scott, Ph.D., Vice President, Applied Psychological Techniques, Inc.
- Dean Stamoulis, Ph.D., Managing Director, Executive Assessment Practice Leader for the Americas, Russell Reynolds Associates

Special Features

Each volume contains a host of actual case studies, sample materials, tips, and cautionary notes. Issues pertaining to globalization, technology, and key executive points are highlighted throughout.

Titles in the Talent Management Essentials series:

Designing and Implementing Global Selection Systems

Ann Marie Ryan and
Nancy Tippins

⊗WILEY-BLACKWELL

A John Wiley & Sons, Ltd., Publication

This edition first published 2009
© 2009 Ann Marie Ryan and Nancy Tippins

Blackwell Publishing was acquired by John Wiley & Sons in February 2007. Blackwell's publishing program has been merged with Wiley's global Scientific, Technical, and Medical business to form Wiley-Blackwell.

Registered Office
John Wiley & Sons Ltd, The Atrium, Southern Gate, Chichester, West Sussex, PO19 8SQ, United Kingdom

Editorial Offices
350 Main Street, Malden, MA 02148-5020, USA
9600 Garsington Road, Oxford, OX4 2DQ, UK
The Atrium, Southern Gate, Chichester, West Sussex, PO19 8SQ, UK

For details of our global editorial offices, for customer services, and for information about how to apply for permission to reuse the copyright material in this book please see our website at www.wiley.com/wiley-blackwell.

The right of Ann Marie Ryan and Nancy Tippins to be identified as the author of this work has been asserted in accordance with the Copyright, Designs and Patents Act 1988.

Wiley also publishes its books in a variety of electronic formats. Some content that appears in print may not be available in electronic books.

Designations used by companies to distinguish their products are often claimed as trademarks. All brand names and product names used in this book are trade names, service marks, trademarks or registered trademarks of their respective owners. The publisher is not associated with any product or vendor mentioned in this book. This publication is designed to provide accurate and authoritative information in regard to the subject matter covered. It is sold on the understanding that the publisher is not engaged in rendering professional services. If professional advice or other expert assistance is required, the services of a competent professional should be sought.

Library of Congress Cataloging-in-Publication Data

Ryan, Ann Marie.
 Designing and implementing global selection systems / Ann Marie Ryan and Nancy Tippins.
   p.   cm. – (Talent management essentials)
   Includes bibliographical references and index.
   ISBN 978-1-4051-7991-1 (hardcover : alk. paper) – ISBN 978-1-4051-7992-8 (pbk. : alk. paper)
 1. Employee selection.   2. International business enterprises–Employees.   3. International business enterprises–Personnel management.   4. Employment in foreign countries.   I. Tippins, Nancy.   II. Title.
   HF5549.5.S38R93   2009
   658.3'112–dc22

                                                                                            2008051436

A catalogue record for this book is available from the British Library.

Icon in Case Scenario boxes © Kathy Konkle/istockphoto.com

Set in 10.5 on 12.5 pt Minion by SNP Best-set Typesetter Ltd., Hong Kong
Printed in Singapore by Ho Printing Singapore Pte Ltd

1   2009

Contents

Series Editor's Preface

The *Talent Management Essentials* series presents state-of-the-art thinking on critical talent management topics ranging from global staffing, to career pathing, to engagement, to executive staffing, to performance management, to mentoring, to real-time leadership development. Authored by leading authorities and scholars on their respective topics, each volume offers state-of-the-art thinking and the epitome of evidence-based practice. These authors bring to their books an incredible wealth of experience working with small, large, public and private organizations, as well as keen insights into the science and best practices associated with talent management.

Written succinctly and without superfluous "fluff," this series provides powerful and practical treatments of essential talent topics critical to maximizing individual and organizational health, well-being and effectiveness. The books, taken together, provide a comprehensive and contemporary treatment of approaches, tools, and techniques associated with Talent Management. The goal of the series is to produce focused, prescriptive volumes that translate the data- and practice-based knowledge of I/O psychology and Organizational Behavior into practical, "how to" advice for dealing with cutting-edge organizational issues and problems.

Talent Management Essentials is a comprehensive, practitioner-oriented series of "best practices" for the busy solution-oriented manager, executive, HR leader, and consultant. And, in its application of evidence-based practice, this series will also appeal to professors, executive MBA students, and graduate students in Organizational Behavior, Human Resources Management, and I/O Psychology.

Steven Rogelberg

Introduction

Acme Corporation, a large, US-based multinational corporation (MNC), recently developed a process to select entry-level sales representatives at its US locations. The process lasts a half day and is composed of (a) a use of information test that measures the ability to read and interpret verbal and numerical information, (b) an analogies test that measures the ability to reason verbally, (c) a personality test that evaluates personality characteristics related to the sales position, (d) a video-based situational judgment test that assesses judgment in sales-related situations, and (e) a structured interview. The process is administered and scored electronically via the internet. Consequently, all applicants get the same instructions and time limit, and their responses are consistently evaluated. The interview is given only to those who pass the tests. At least three individuals must be interviewed before an offer is made.

The selection process has been very successful in identifying capable sales reps in the US from a US applicant pool. The sales figures of sales representatives hired with this process are 10% greater in the first two years than sales reps who were hired with a series of unstructured interviews. Because the process has been so well-received in the US, the Global Vice President of Sales has decided to extend it world-wide and use it to select sales representatives in over 40 countries. The Vice President announces the new selection process at the Global Sales Meeting and contracts with a vendor to translate the tests and interview into the necessary languages. Once the translations are done, the tools are sent to the Sales organization in each country. Within a week, the Global Vice President has calls and emails from around the globe!

- Country 1 has been using a different sales selection process for five years that was developed by a consultant in that country. According to the VP in Country 1, the process works fine. VP-1 wants evidence that the US approach to selection is better than the one he is currently using.
- Country 2 has never used formal selection tools. Most hiring is based on educational credentials, and even those with degrees from prestigious universities usually need a contact within the organization. VP-2 argues that changing the hiring process would offend many of the current employees and possibly signal that the company is no longer a good employer for people with a good education.
- VP-3 sends an email explaining that in Africa, few people are familiar with the concept of analogies because this type of test is not taught or used in the educational system. If the company wants to hire anyone in Africa, the analogies component has got to go.
- Most of the VPs outside the US (OUS) are irate about the Use of Information Test because several of the tables included dollar figures. The translators left the dollars signs in, and the VPs believe the dollar signs reflect an offensive level of US-centrism. The Global VP quickly had the dollar signs replaced with the currency used in a specific country. Now some of the OUS VPs are complaining that the figures make no sense. For example, at an exchange rate of $1 to approximately 107 Japanese yen, the value of some items in the table are ridiculously low. A truck that costs $50,000 in the US now costs 50,000 yen, which is about US$500.
- Many of the OUS VPs took the Situational Judgment Test (SJT), which presents common sales situations and asks the test taker to select one of four possible responses as the best action to take and one as the worst. Many performed poorly, suggested some of the situations were not relevant to sales jobs, and contended that the appropriate response in the US is not the appropriate response in their countries. For example, one of the situations features a sales representative who has a new client she would like to get to know better. One of the response options is to invite the client to lunch; however, inviting a stranger to lunch is simply not done in some

countries. In another scenario, a subordinate speaks angrily to his supervisor. Because such behavior is unacceptable in his country, VP-6 believes the SJT cannot work there.

- The translations appear to be an abysmal failure. In some countries, VPs are pointing out grammar mistakes and ambiguity in the tests. The questions in the interview are stilted and awkward. HR in those countries expresses concern that applicants will not work for a company that could not even write a test or interview well in their language. Upon inspection, it appears that some of the translations have resulted in much more difficult text than others. In some cases, the translator added explanatory information that may have made the question easier. Many managers are complaining that the tests and interviews are not available in their language or dialect. For example, India has 18 official languages, and many of these have dialects. The individual who translated the test spoke Punjab and ignored the other languages. Also, the VPs from all the Latin American countries sign a joint letter complaining about the translations and pointing out that the Castilian Spanish, which the translators used, doesn't always work in Central and South America.

- The VPs in the various Sales divisions in the US corner the Global Vice President at a meeting. They express concern that he distributed their selection tools that worked so well to people in other countries, many of whom have no experience with formal selection programs and were given no training in maintaining the security of the test materials.

- VP-7 protests that the personality tests will not work in her country. Sales representatives in Country 7 are not outgoing in the same way American sales representatives are. Consequently, their scores on the personality tests are not going to reflect their true characteristics.

- There is an immediate request for a version of the selection system to be used in Country 8 in South America, where a new office is to be opened in a month's time. Country 8 was not on the list of countries considered when developing the system because there is no other sales office there currently.

- Although a poor country historically, Country 9 has a growing middle class that is hungry for the consumer goods Acme sells. However, competition for employees from this educated, middle class is fierce. VP-9 is confident he will not find enough capable employees to fill his jobs if the company requires he meet the new standards. In contrast, the VPs of many other poorer countries believe that many of their fellow citizens are smart but under-educated and consequently, they will not do well on the selection process although many would make competent sales reps.

- Several other VPs from emerging nations also protest the new selection procedures for various reasons. VPs in several countries want to know where they will get the computers to administer the tests and video equipment to administer the SJT, particularly when the tests must be administered in far-flung provinces distant from the company headquarters. Other VPs want to know from where the electricity to run the computers will come. Others are confident their applicants are smart enough to pass the tests but probably lack computer skills to take the tests.

- VPs in several countries note that they may not see an applicant until an offer is made. An agency recruits applicants, and all interviews except the last one take place over the telephone. These VPs want to know if they can reverse the order and test applicants only after they have passed all interviews.

- The VPs in some countries announce they are not going to use the process because it violates the laws of their country. In one country, the tests cannot be used unless there is a validity study that demonstrates how the process relates to job performance. In another, there must be strict safeguards in protecting private information such as test scores.

- The VP in Country 10 cannot implement the system until he negotiates with his local Work Councils. To do that, he needs detailed descriptions of the tests and interviews and a statement of what they measure written in his language.

- Several VPs have suggested that they need evidence of the selection system's effectiveness in their locations before they implement it. They are willing to provide scores from their local performance evaluation system so the Global VP can have a psychologist conduct a research study statistically linking the scores and the job performance. Unfortunately, the operational measures of sales performance differ from country to country.

- The VP in Country 11 is worried that the process of testing individuals in her location and comparing them to applicants in

Countries 12 and 13, who will use the same language version of the test, is inherently unfair. The labor market in Country 11 is such that applicants for sales jobs have very little formal schooling relative to the degree holders applying for the same job in Countries 12 and 13. She will use the tests if she is allowed to set a cut score that is different from that of her neighbors.

- The video-based SJT was filmed in North Dakota in the winter. One of the scenarios shows a supervisor admonishing an employee to wear gloves when she touches metal structures outdoors. In another, employees are complaining to the supervisor that the buildings are not sufficiently heated. One sales manager from a tropical country is not sure what the white stuff on the ground is and wonders if it is fire-retarding foam. Others ask if those scenarios can just be skipped because they deal with issues that are not relevant to their climate.

- In some countries, the Sales Representative job is very different from the consultative sales job found in the U.S. In some countries, the Sales Representative job is an "order taker" job. In others, it is door-to-door sales or retail sales. In some countries, sales representatives only write proposals responding to RFPs. A number of VPs representing these countries have asked how the test can work for these kinds of jobs as well as the consultative sales positions.

- A few VPs are unhappy because they were not consulted beforehand, and they are not inclined to buy into a selection process that they feel has been dictated by the U.S.

- The HR Department is upset in general. The staffing and recruiting teams in many locations do not have the skill to administer the test or interpret it. Their clients, the Sales Departments, are calling with questions they can't answer.

Clearly, our Global Vice President of Sales has a few problems to solve! What seemed like such a good idea has turned into a nightmare. The task of implementing a global selection process is not quite as easy as it seems. Designing selection tools for global use is not simply a matter of transferring existing methods from one setting to another. The global selection system must take into account the cultural opportunities and constraints from the start. The crux of the challenge is how to maintain standardization of policies and procedures while incorporating sensitivity to local culture and norms.

The purpose of this book is to help you understand the problems that may accompany the introduction of global selection programs and offer possible solutions for your situation so that you can avoid the same problems our Global VP has on his plate. We don't intend to scare you away from creating a good, global selection program. There are solutions to the problems presented here, and the rewards can be stunning.

This book is written specifically for the manager responsible for global selection programs. This book is not intended to be a "how to" manual for the development and validation of tests and interviews or a technical treatise on global testing for industrial and organizational psychologists and other testing professionals. Rather, this book is a guide for the manager who oversees technical testing experts or who contracts with vendors for those tasks. We want to inform you so that you can make intelligent decisions, ask your experts the right questions, and ensure your management team addresses these questions appropriately while implementing a global staffing system.

The goals of this book are to provide you with the following:

- The basic principles of employee selection.
- Insights as to the challenges of globally standardized selection systems.
- Knowledge as to how to address those challenges effectively.
- Decision aids and examples to assist you in making the best choices regarding selection system development and implementation.

The book is organized into seven chapters:

Chapter 1: Challenges in Developing and Implementing Global Selection Systems

Chapter 1 describes the challenges and dilemmas faced when using selection tools globally. As the Global Vice President of Sales in our scenario now knows, there are many problems when developing and implementing global selection systems, and this chapter highlights many of the typical ones. We believe that well-informed managers can avoid some problems and identify effective solutions for others.

Chapter 2: Characteristics of Good Selection Systems

Chapter 2 provides a primer on the basics of what makes for a good selection tool. We take the point of view that effective hiring occurs when selection procedures are job-related and administered consistently so that all candidates are treated equitably. Throughout the book, we emphasize that the selection tools should be based on a thoughtful and thorough development process and should predict job performance, turnover, or other outcomes important to the organization. These basic principles of good selection apply regardless of where the process is used – the small family business in one small town or the large multinational corporation (MNC) doing business in the major cities of the world. This chapter will provide an overview of how good selection tools are developed that will help you evaluate your own selection processes.

Chapter 3: Cultural Differences and Their Impact on Selection Systems

Chapter 3 explores what is meant by cultural differences and how these differences affect employee selection. Many times these differences are not apparent or their implications for selection have not been carefully considered. This chapter will highlight common cultural differences and discuss their impact on selection processes. We hope that by being aware of these cultural differences, you can design selection processes that take them into account.

Chapter 4: Legal, Economic, and Other Considerations

Virtually all modern, ethical companies intend to comply with the laws of the countries in which they do business. Chapter 4 provides a very brief overview of some of the implications of different employment laws and the effects of different labor markets for selection system design. Although this is not an exhaustive explanation of the labor laws across all countries, we have highlighted the legal issues that arise in many countries. You will need to rely on your company's legal counsel for specific advice, but we want to attune you to the questions that need to be raised. A selection process cannot be effective unless it fits the legal and labor environment of all the countries in which it will be used.

Chapter 5: Best Practices in the Design of Global Selection Systems

Chapter 5 describes the best practices in designing global selection systems. This chapter will walk you through each step of the development process and highlight when you must consider local customs, laws, and practices. Common pitfalls and good solutions will be presented.

Chapter 6: Best Practices in the Implementation of Global Selection Systems

Chapter 6 describes best practices in implementing global selection systems as well as ways to monitor a tool that is in place. A well-designed selection system may not be effective if the implementation is careless, and a carefully implemented set of selection tools may not remain effective without continual review and corrective action. The chapter is intended to guide you through the implementation process.

Chapter 7: Final Thoughts

Chapter 7 concludes the book by providing some closing thoughts on future trends and challenges.

Format of the Chapters

Throughout the chapters, the sidebars contain examples and summaries that help illustrate the text. We end each chapter with a set of questions (Think about this!) to help you evaluate where you stand with regard to designing and implementing a global selection system. We suggest you use these in your discussions with those tasked with system design and implementation and that you consider them in planning your system.

Chapter 1

Challenges in Developing and Implementing Global Selection Systems

The development and implementation of global selection systems have benefits as well as challenges. (See Figure 1.1.) When standardization occurs, numerous advantages to the organization can be gained and the costs related to employee selection greatly reduced. (See box below.) A globally consistent selection program enhances talent management and aids the organization in deploying human capital where needed by providing accurate, job-relevant information on applicants and employees. In addition, common staffing practices help communicate the organizational culture to applicants in a consistent manner around the world. However, developing a globally standardized selection system is a challenging task that requires careful thought and planning. In this chapter, we will provide an overview of the common challenges in this type of undertaking, each of which is explored in depth in subsequent chapters. The challenges that are discussed below are based on the experiences of large multinational companies (MNCs). Some of the examples come from a study of six major MNCs (IBM, P&G, Agilent, Shell, Dow, and Motorola) that developed selection systems for global use (1). Other information comes from our own work with MNCs based in the USA and Europe.

1

(a)

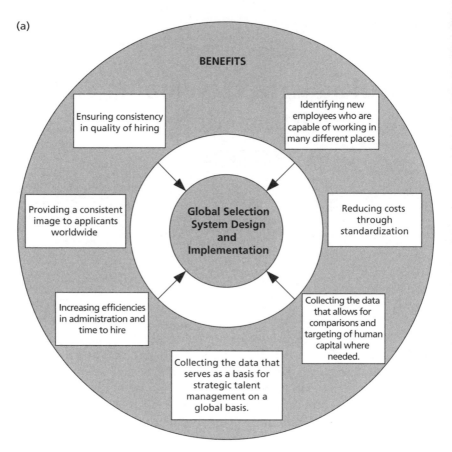

Figure 1.1 Benefits and Challenges of a Global Selection System

(b)

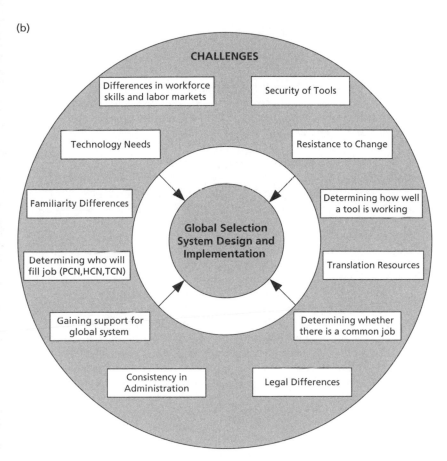

Figure 1.1 *Continued*

Good to Know:
Costs and Efficiencies in Global Selection Systems

Selection systems have three primary sources of costs: (a) development, (b) implementation, and (c) ongoing operational use.

Development includes development of tests, interview protocols, and accompanying materials, and validation (i.e., the process of demonstrating these tools do indeed help select the best candidates). Many of these costs are fixed, and to the extent that this effort is minimized or the same or similar instruments are used in multiple places, significant savings accrue. However, a few development costs such as translations are specific to a location and recur in each new culture.

Implementation includes activities such as loading assessments on computerized administration platforms, printing tests, training administrators and interviewers, communicating with users and hiring managers, etc. Because many of these activities are generally repeated many times, they can be costly. Again, when a product is used multiple times, the cost savings can be significant. For example, developing one interviewer training program for global deployment is much cheaper than developing a different one in every country.

Operational use includes activities associated with actually administering, scoring, and using selection tools. Most of these activities are performed locally so there are few opportunities for savings from activities like administration, scoring, data management, etc. Nevertheless, common systems and policies can be used. For example, one database that is used for a repository for applicant information is cheaper than twenty.

Challenges in Selection System Development for Global Use

As our Global VP of Sales in our introductory scenario discovered, many challenges can arise in developing a selection system for global use. To address these challenges, we have organized this chapter around a set of questions that will focus your attention on some of the critical decisions to be made before embarking on a global selection system. (See Figure 1.2 for a summary of the questions.) While answering these questions is often difficult, failing to ask and address them can lead to catastrophe.

Do the Leaders in My Organization see the World as Converging or Diverging?

Whether you even consider the possibility of developing a global selection system depends a lot on where you stand on *convergence* and *divergence* (2). (See Figure 1.3 for an illustration.) Consider the following case study.

     Case Scenario

The corporate HR Director and the corporate Manufacturing Director are debating whether to implement a global selection system for engineers in all of the manufacturing plants or to allow each country to develop its own system tailored to the location's special needs. The Manufacturing Director feels that a good engineer needs to have the same skills no matter where in the world you go, and he wants the HR group to come up with a useful web-screening tool and interview protocol that can be implemented worldwide. The HR Director believes that cultural differences mean that different skills and characteristics are needed to perform the engineering job in different countries, and therefore each region needs to come up with its own system.

Some, like the Manufacturing Director in the case above, subscribe to a view of convergence: Societies are growing more alike, and there is an increasing interchange of ideas, goods and people. Consequently, there are many universals that transcend national borders and affect the ways in which business is conducted. Similarly, competitive pressures often lead organizations to eventually adopt universal best practices. Others, like the HR Director in the vignette, feel that the tendency toward convergence is overstated and that local culture still has significant effects on how work is done. Employee preferences and practice differences related to culture are still very important (3, 4). Others note that to be competitive, products and services have to be "fine tuned" for the local customers (5).

Figure 1.2 Critical Questions to Answer before Designing a Global Selection System

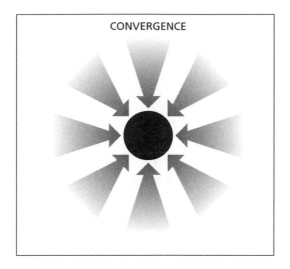

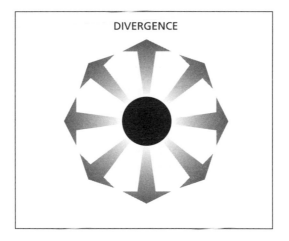

Figure 1.3 Convergence – Divergence

Of course, elements of both convergence and divergence exist. Some things are converging into one universal practice – for example, communications via the Internet. At the same time, numerous local customs remain firmly entrenched. Whether your organization is already moving toward convergence in staffing systems, feels convergence is an inevitability, or considers divergence too great to allow for standardization in selection, is a question you will have to explore and answer. We hope this book will provide you with guidance in doing so.

The pressures for global integration or local responsiveness vary according to many factors, including the industry, the function, task, and the organizational level. Within a single organization, some things may be converging; others diverging. For example, the design and marketing of consumer goods may need to be tailored to customs of a region while computer hardware and software share common features across national boundaries. Policies may be set internationally but sales promotions may be designed locally. Human resource (HR) management is frequently considered the most local of functions (5). Often, an organization that has global processes in manufacturing and finance still has differentiated HR practices, including different selection tools and processes in different locations.

One key to success in implementing a global selection system is determining if there is enough convergence to make it worthwhile using a similar system across locations. Even if you believe there is evidence of sufficient convergence, it may be a challenge to convince others in your organization that similarities in jobs and staffing processes exist. Some of your associates will focus on the differences rather than the commonalities. Also, many will have a vested interest in divergent staffing.

Is There Support for a Global System?

Garnering support for developing and implementing a global system is a first hurdle that must be overcome before anything else can happen. Individuals are rightly proud of their cultural identity and may be reluctant to follow a system "imposed" from elsewhere. Further, many individuals may feel that local responsiveness requires a different selection process in each location. Incorporating stakeholder views and gaining support will be introduced in Chapter 2 and expanded upon in Chapters 5 and 6.

Is There a Common Job?

One of the first decisions you must make is whether there is a common job across locations and cultures. Often, this decision is made unconsciously or with minimal thought or systematic investigation.

However, just because jobs have a similar title across locations, you should not automatically assume them to be identical. Conversely, if a job is labeled differently and has different pay rates in different countries, that by no means indicates it is not essentially the same job. From a selection perspective, two jobs must have similar knowledge, skills, abilities and other characteristics (KSAOs for short) requirements to warrant the same tool. One selection process can be used for two jobs regardless of title if the tasks performed or the KSAOs required are similar. For example, both warehouse product pickers and customer order takers need to be able to read product numbers without error so a checking simulation could be used for both. In Chapter 2 we will discuss the process of deciding whether enough commonalities exist to use the same selection system or even just some of the same components of a system; in Chapter 5 we will describe specific issues related to making those judgments when looking globally.

Who Will Fill the Job?

Another early decision is determining whether the job will be filled locally, regionally, or from further afield. While lower-level positions often draw candidates from the local labor markets, higher-level positions may be filled by locals or expatriates from corporate headquarters or other facilities.

Definitions

Expatriate: Citizen of one country working in another country
Parent Country National (PCN): Citizen of the MNC's headquarters country who is sent to foreign positions
Host Country National (HCN): Citizen of the country in which he/she is working
Third Country National (TCN): Citizen of one country, working in a second country and working for an MNC headquartered in a third country (e.g., a manager from Germany working in China for Ford Motor Company, which is headquartered in the USA)
Inpatriation: Developing HCNs and TCNs through transfers to the headquarters country

Source: (6).

Your applicant source affects your selection system design in several ways. First, the amount of education and experience possessed by your new hires determines how much training you will need to provide and how you should organize the work. Second, the selection system must be designed around the requirements of the job and is determined to some extent by the source of applicants. For example, if the candidates for a job are expatriates from your own company, you will have a lot of information about the applicant and so your selection process may focus on indicators of past performance inside the company. In contrast, if you are hiring locals in a foreign country to perform the job, you may not know how to evaluate their educational credentials and experience in terms of knowledge and skills, and you may want to evaluate them with a selection tool that provides information in terms you understand. If some jobs are always filled with expatriates, then certain KSAOs do not need to be assessed. You probably don't need to evaluate technical knowledge for a plant manager position if it is always filled from the ranks of managers in the headquarters location.

Why might an organization decide to bring in expatriate managers? In some circumstances, such a decision is made without much thought. However, the decision to use expatriates is often a conscious one when organizations wish to achieve aims such as those noted in the box below.

Best Practices and Common Pitfalls Using Expatriates

Best Practices
When implemented strategically, using expatriates can:

- Transfer knowledge from one location to other locations.
- Maintain informal social control over branches/subsidiaries.
- Provide opportunities for the development of high potential managers.
- Address shortages of qualified labor pools in a host country (7, 8).

Common Pitfall
Using expatriates can:

- Be based on tradition or expedience rather than a thoughtful, strategic decision.

The table on page 12 illustrates different views on the use of PCN, HCN, and TCN employees. Recognize the pros and cons of taking a more ethnocentric, polycentric, regiocentric, or geocentric approach and choose what is best for where your organization is today – or where you soon plan to be.

Reliance on expatriates varies from firm to firm, country to country, and time to time. For example, though many believe that Japanese MNCs rely more on expatriates than European and US firms, that tendency appears to have declined (11).

Traditional expatriate assignments involve relocation of the employee and his/her family and usually last significant periods of time. While estimates vary, 20 percent of foreign assignments are terminated early (12). When there are shortages of individuals willing to accept the disruption associated with international assignments, it is necessary to rethink strategies to find and place qualified workers.

There tends to be fierce competition for individuals who have knowledge of successful business practices in emerging markets such as China and India. The pool of available and qualified individuals is further reduced because of the growing number of firms needing international managers. Overall, demand is high, and supply is low.

Examples:
Alternatives to Traditional Expatriate Assignments

- short-term assignments
- international business travelers, often called frequent flyers
- commuter assignments, in which the employee goes home regularly (e.g., Eurocommuting)
- virtual assignments, in which the worker performs the job remotely through technological aids
- new hires who seek and volunteer for foreign work experiences

Source: (13).

Approach	Description
Ethnocentric (focused on headquarters culture)	• Uses PCNs • Relies on headquarters policies and procedures • Minimizes differences across cultures
Polycentric (focused on multiple local cultures)	• Uses HCNs • Orients program to individual country • Lacks global uniformity • Recognizes cultural differences
Regiocentric (focused on one region that may incorporate multiple cultures)	• Uses TCNs and HCNs • Selects within a region • Creates uniformity within a region
Geocentric (focused on the entire world across all regions and cultures)	• Uses PCNs, HCNs, and TCNs

Sources: (2, 9, 10).

In sum, a key challenge will be identifying what approach you will take in filling positions at all levels of the organization. The approach that works best at higher levels of the organization may not be appropriate for lower levels, given differences in talent availability and comparability across locations as well as the cost effectiveness of

Pro	Con
• Optimizes control • Transfers organizational culture to other locations • Develops headquarters employees • Provides human resources when there is a lack of local qualified staff	• Generally costs more • Risks expatriate failure • Sometimes ignores local culture and needs • May fail to take into account possible legislative restrictions on visas and work permits • Uses more short-term appointments • Limits development of HCNs
• Develops local employees • Costs less than PCNs • Depends on longer-term appointments which are usually more efficient • Helps when there is a lack of knowledge of local labor market or languages	• Provides less control • Risks HCN failure • Does not promote familiarity with headquarters • Does not build international professional skill • Can be limited by local laws requiring company to hire certain numbers of HCNs
• Provides a neutral alternative • Expands labor pool within company	• Can be limited by legislative restrictions on work permits and visas • Relies on shorter-term appointments which are usually less efficient
• Selects best regardless of nationality • Promotes consistency across countries and regions • Can be sensitive to local cultures	• Can be limited in use by local regulations regarding hiring foreign workers • Requires more coordination of human resource programs

using PCNs, HCNs and TCNs at lower levels. Another challenge once an approach is chosen is determining if it can be successfully carried out, given labor availability within your organization and in the locales where you have hiring needs. We'll address the issue of labor markets in more detail in Chapter 4.

What Will Be Selection System Content?

Determining what to measure in a selection system as well as how to measure what's important presents many questions and challenges. You must decide if you will measure reading, math, or communication skills, and you must choose a format such as paper-and-pencil tests, interview, or work sample. There are also decisions to be made regarding question type – word problems, analogies, comparisons, etc. and response format – short answers, multiple choice, essays, etc. The cultural contexts in which the system is used will affect these choices. For example, because straight translations do not necessarily result in equivalent language, you may need to avoid questions that depend on understanding the nuances of meaning. A word that is very easy in English may be translated to a very difficult word in Chinese. Sometimes, a word does not have a comparable word in another language. For instance, many tropical countries have no words for boots. Some question content may be offensive in one culture. If the meat of some animals is not eaten in some countries, a test question that references eating that meat may distract the applicant unnecessarily. Some content may be considered unacceptably intrusive in some cultures. You may offend an applicant if you ask in an interview how he or she feels about past supervisors. In Chapters 3 and 5, we will discuss these specific challenges in determining tool content and effective ways to handle them.

How Will You Determine if a Tool is Working Well?

Establishing the effectiveness of a selection tool is a difficult task to undertake in just one country, and the logistical challenges increase substantially when the evaluation involves multiple countries and cultures. The process of ensuring scores or ratings have the same meaning anywhere in the world is perhaps even more difficult. The user of a selection tool must compare scores across countries and determine if differences are due to the abilities of the sample of candidates taking the selection tool, the culture, or the content of the assessment. Chapter 5 focuses on how to address this particular challenge.

Definition:
"What Is a Test?"

The term "test" typically conjures up images of #2 pencils and bubble sheets, strict time limits, and "one right answer." However, the term "test" actually refers to any method of evaluating an individual's knowledge, skills, abilities, or other personal characteristics. In the US legal system, tests are anything used to make an employment decision about a candidate, and this definition is widely adopted by professionals involved in selection system design. Tests can be as simple as a quick resume review or as complex as a demonstration of appropriate wiring for a piece of equipment. Tests can be informal and involve asking individuals to demonstrate a skill such as "develop an Excel spreadsheet" or "give a presentation." Or, tests can be standardized sets of questions with definite correct answers that measure a defined scope of knowledge. Tests can be given in many modes – paper-and-pencil, orally, or computer-based. They can be administered in proctored or unproctored environments. Tests also vary in how closely they reflect actual job tasks. A test can be low fidelity and resemble tasks performed on the job (e.g., a test composed of written or video scenarios of an interpersonal conflict followed by multiple choice questions) or high fidelity and identical to tasks performed on the job (e.g., a work sample test that asks a person to perform an actual job task such as troubleshoot a piece of equipment) or somewhere in between (e.g., a role play in which the person does what he/she would do in such a conflict situation). Interviews are in essence orally administered tests. Resume screens, application reviews, or past performance ratings used in promotion infer skills or knowledge from education or experience and are also considered tests.

Why the fuss? Knowing that all of these tools are really "tests" is important to understanding that the same principles for good construction and proper use apply to *all* types of selection tools. Too often we see organizations worry about the quality of traditional multiple choice tests and not hold the rest of the selection system to the same standards, when all components should be.

Challenges in Selection System Implementation across Boundaries

Developing a global system is only half the battle; the second half involves implementing a staffing process on a global basis. There are a number of problems that you should expect and be prepared to handle. Below we briefly list the most important questions to address. They are all discussed more fully in the following chapters.

How Can You Minimize Resistance to Change?

Resistance to a new selection process needs to be investigated and evaluated, and then overcome. In a global context, there can be many reasons for resisting change. For example, Dow Chemical found that "cultural unacceptability" was mentioned by hiring managers and HR as a reason to not institute an online application tool; yet pilot testing of the tool had demonstrated it was universally positively viewed by applicants (14). In other cases, resistance arises from legitimate barriers to effective implementation such as lack of equipment or skills to administer the selection process or legal impediments.

The source of resistance can also result from the characteristics of the selection system. For example, some people may not like the type of selection procedure used; others may not like the standards that define qualification. Resistance does not always stem from the characteristics of the selection system; they can arise when local hiring managers and HR staff feel that a system was imposed on them rather than being created with their active involvement in its design and development. Chapter 6 covers how to effectively market a new system to stakeholders.

How will you Deal with Employment Laws that Differ Country by Country?

As we will point out in detail in Chapter 4, employment laws do differ across countries, and it is imperative that you understand those laws that apply to you in developing and implementing global systems and determine whether constraints proposed by those in a location are driven by law or custom. In the study of six MNCs mentioned earlier, Agilent Technologies and IBM found that in their efforts to create globally standardized systems, they often encountered beliefs that current methods could not be changed because they were "legally required" (14). Further probing at both organizations found that these procedures were more "the way it has always been done" than something that was legally mandated.

Example:
A Unique Law

In South Africa, Section 8 of the Employment Equity Act (EEA) 55/1998 prohibits the use of psychological testing and other similar assessments unless the tool: (i) has been scientifically shown to be valid and reliable; (ii) can be applied to all employees; and (iii) is not biased against any employee or group. This is a much more stringent requirement than is to be found almost anywhere on the globe. Equal employment laws do differ from country to country, and in designing a global system, you must take this into account.

How Will you Address Differences in Familiarity with and Attitudes Toward Specific Tools Across Countries?

Familiarity with various selection tools differs from location to location. For example, a study of selection practices of 959 organizations from 20 countries documented variability in what types of selection tools tend to be most widely used in different countries (15). We will provide more detail on this in Chapter 3. Any attempt to institute a new selection system on a global basis needs to investigate and recognize the differences in familiarity with tools across cultures. Familiarity is important for several reasons. First, familiarity may affect how well an applicant does in the selection process. Someone who has never worked an analogy may be just as smart as a person who has worked many such problems, but the applicant who is unfamiliar with analogies may score lower due to lack of familiarity. Second, applicants may dislike tools containing question formats with which they are unfamiliar and feel that they are disadvantaged in the hiring process. These perceptions may translate into less attraction to the hiring organization and willingness to pursue employment. Third, unfamiliar types of selection tools may not be trusted by local managers, greatly increasing the efforts needed to implement the new processes. Finally, in some cultures, any kind of testing is neither common nor valued. Again, you will have to explain what you are doing and why you are doing it, and then demonstrate the effectiveness of the selection system to convince local managers of the value of a new selection system. In Chapter 6 we'll discuss specific ways to address unfamiliarity with testing and item types.

How will you Ensure the Security of Assessment Materials?

Cultural acceptability of sharing selection process information varies too (16, 17, 18). In some countries, employees and applicants are careful to maintain the security of materials. In other countries, materials may be widely disseminated regardless of prohibitions against doing so. Successful global implementation requires considering the likelihood that hiring tools will be compromised – and finding ways to safeguard against this. In Chapter 6, we will discuss this issue in more detail.

How can Consistency in the Administration of the Process be Achieved?

Standardized conditions help ensure each applicant has the same opportunity to display his or her skills in a selection process. However, ensuring consistent administration is not always easy. Proctored testing in appropriate environments may not be possible in some locations. Using an Internet-based platform for administering tools may ensure consistent standards in locations where the Internet connections are good, but not in those places where connections are sporadic or access is limited. The importance of understanding the staffing environment will be covered extensively in Chapters 2 and 6.

Example:
3M's Staffing Environment in India

3M employs over 1,000 individuals in many locations across India. Although all staffing is carried out from Bangalore, sourcing firms are used to identify qualified candidates at each location. These sourcing firms review resumes but do not administer testing as an early screen. Consequently, 3M defers testing until candidates are interviewed in Bangalore, resulting in a selection process that is quite different from the process in locations where screening via computerized testing can take place early on. Even then, testing cannot be consistently administered as interviews are often conducted in hotel lobbies rather than in locations where standardized testing is facilitated.

How Will You Find Translated Tools or the Resources for Translation?

We have seen many an instance where an organization has a great tool in place in one locale and desires to adopt it worldwide only to find that there are not versions in all the languages for all the locales in which they will be hiring. There is also an under-appreciation for how much a high-quality translation process costs. For organizations doing business in multiple languages, budgeting for this aspect of the process is essential. Managing translations of tools will be covered in Chapter 5.

How Will You Acquire Needed Technology when Familiarity and Availability Varies from Country to Country?

While the Internet has certainly played a unifying role in businesses globally, the average applicant may not have the same resources or familiarity with technology as employees have at their offices in the organization. Access still varies considerably throughout the globe, as does the speed of transmission and the quality of equipment. Designing a global selection system requires careful consideration of the extent to which the technological capacities of *applicants* in all locations match the selection system requirements and the organization is willing to invest in providing needed technology for applicant use. Chapters 5 and 6 will touch upon addressing this important issue.

How Will Differences in Workforce Skill Levels and Labor Markets Across Countries Affect Your Efforts?

Even with a well-developed and well-supported selection system ready to be fully implemented in multiple locations, the usefulness of the selection system may be in question when the number of available applicants with the needed skills varies from place to place. For example, in countries with high unemployment rates and a large number of qualified applicants, a good selection system that identifies candidates with the appropriate skill sets may be welcomed. In contrast, when employment rates are high, there may be an insufficient number of applicants, and a selection system that further reduces the applicant pool may be more unacceptable than unqualified employees. In different locations, rates of illiteracy, enrollment in higher education, and expenditures per pupil by educational systems vary considerably, leaving an organization with large differences in numbers of potentially qualified applicants across locations. No matter how good the selection system is, applicants who possess the fundamental skills required by the job are necessary for it to be an effective part of the overall hiring process. The challenges insufficient labor pools present will be discussed in greater detail in Chapter 4.

Organizations may also differ in how they respond to diminished labor supplies. For example, a common US response to labor shortages is to bring more foreign workers into the USA or to send work offshore, while organizations in Hong Kong typically focus on internal strategies for the retention and development of existing employees (19). Because labor uncertainty is handled differently in different places, local managers will respond to selection systems in different ways. A highly selective process will not be well received when a labor shortage already makes it difficult to fill positions. A less stringent selection process will be of little value when qualified applicants are plentiful.

Let's return to our Acme Global VP of Sales and discuss how he might have used the ideas in this chapter to avoid some of the problems he faced. It is clear from the scenario that in general HR practices at Acme are fairly differentiated by locale, and that many of the organization's executive leaders neither see convergence occurring nor support a global system. If our Acme VP had greater awareness of his environment upfront, he might have moved more cautiously in thinking that a good selection process in one locale would be embraced globally.

Second, our hapless Global VP of Sales could have won more people over if he had armed himself with data to support treating the sales job as equivalent worldwide. Without agreement on the commonality of the job, he cannot successfully argue for a global selection system. Providing evidence of an equivalent sales rep job and obtaining agreement on this issue early on would have paved the way for a global system.

Third, the VP could have done some homework on how positions are sourced in each country so that he would be ready for objections related to difficulties in recruiting and administering the tests and interview. Similarly, if the VP had paid attention to variations in who filled the job in each country, he might have adapted his selection process to better fit the applicant population.

Fourth, a plan for evaluation might have gone a long way to reassure the other VPs, some of whom felt disenfranchised by the imposition of the new selection process, that the Global VP's ultimate goal was a selection process that worked.

Each of the challenges that arose – the acceptability of content, the quality of translations, the evidence of tool effectiveness, the legal environment, tool security, technology needs, and administration consistency – will be addressed in the chapters that follow.

Benefits of Global Systems

After reading a chapter on challenges, you may be rethinking your interest in a global selection system! Lest you get discouraged, let us emphasize the many benefits of a global selection process (1):

- Ensuring consistency in quality of hiring.
- Identifying new employees who are capable of working in many different places.
- Providing a consistent image to applicants worldwide.
- Reducing costs through standardization.
- Increasing efficiencies in administration and time to hire.
- Collecting the data that allow for comparisons and the targeting of human capital where needed.
- Collecting the data that serve as a basis for strategic talent management on a global basis.

For your planning and internal discussions, we end each chapter with a list of questions to stimulate your thoughts about your work and labor environment and potential selection systems. You probably won't be able to provide answers to all of these questions when you finish reading each chapter. The answers may take some thought and some investigative work on your part. However, knowing what questions to answer should be part of your planning.

Think about this!

❖ What is the makeup of your current workforce? How many locations? How many languages? How heterogeneous are global operations?

❖ Where will you need workers in the future? What kind? How many?

❖ What are the challenges that face your organization in designing a global selection system?

❖ Where can you achieve cost efficiencies in development, implementation and use via global standardization?

❖ Do you have jobs that share considerable similarities in terms of tasks and KSAOs across locations or is each one unique?

❖ What is the organizational mindset regarding convergence/divergence in practices?

❖ What is your current approach in the use of PCNs, HCNs, and TCNs? What do you wish it to be?

❖ Do you have support for global implementation?

❖ What are your current processes for selection of expatriates and inpatriates? How effective are they?

❖ What are the major sources of resistance to change?

❖ Have you allocated resources toward translation needs?

❖ What are the legal constraints on selection system design in each location?

❖ How familiar are the tools you are considering in the locations of interest?

❖ Have you allocated resources toward ensuring the security of the system?

❖ What are the technology capabilities of the average applicant in each location? Is technology available in each location? Do you have the budget for it?

❖ What is the labor market profile in each location?

❖ What are the constraints on the physical environment for administering the selection system?

References to Chapter 1

1 Wiechmann, Ryan, & Hemingway, 2003.
2 Vance & Paik, 2006.
3 Cunningham & Rowley, 2007.
4 Myloni, Harzing, & Mirza, 2007.
5 Rosenzweig, 2006.

 6 Collings & Scullion, 2006a.
 7 Edstrum & Galbraith, 1977.
 8 Pires, Stanton, & Ostenfeld, 2006.
 9 Shimoni & Bergmann, 2007.
10 Collings & Scullion, 2006b.
11 Tan & Mahoney, 2006.
12 Groh & Allen, 1998.
13 Collings, Scullion, & Morley, 2007.
14 Ryan, Wiechmann, & Hemingway, 2003.
15 Ryan, McFarland, Baron, & Page, 1999.
16 Burns, Davis, Hoshino, & Miller, 1998.
17 Lupton & Chapman, 2002.
18 Rothstein-Fisch, Trumbull, Issac, Daley, & Perez, 2003.
19 Fields, Chan, Akhtar, & Blum, 2006.

Chapter 2

Characteristics of Good Selection Systems

Assumptions of Selection Systems

Most selection specialists work with organizations that are experiencing some level of unhappiness or "pain" over their hiring processes. Either the organization has no selection process, or people in the organization feel the one they have is inadequate. The costs of poor selection systems, whether due to poorer performance, higher training failures, higher turnover, etc., may not be always translated into dollar terms, but they are usually clearly recognized within the organization. Change in a selection system is needed when the desire to get the right people in the job is not being met.

For over a century, the question of what makes a good tool for selecting employees has been the focus of attention of workplace psychologists. While jobs, organizations, and societies have undergone substantial changes in the past 100+ years, the basic goal of employee selection systems has not changed much: identify applicants who possess the *k*nowledge, *s*kills, *a*bilities, and *o*ther characteristics that are required to perform the job tasks (1) – or KSAOs for short. KSAOs reflect the attributes of the individual necessary to fulfill the job requirements – what is needed to do the job – and are the basis for selection. A critical step in selection system design is clearly defining which KSAOs are needed and which are not.

Whether you are selecting employees from internal or external candidate pools, choosing many new employees or a few, or recruiting from local, national, or global pools, the process of selecting individuals to fill a job is always based on certain assumptions about people and jobs (1). These include:

People Differ in Their KSAOs

You would not need any selection systems if there were no real differences among people in KSAOs. People would be relatively interchangeable, and anyone would do. Occasionally, we come across managers who claim "anyone breathing could fill this job" or "even a monkey could do a good job." However, it is always the case that there are some people who actually do not possess the personal attributes necessary to perform the job well.

Good to Know:
Are KSAOs and Competencies Different?

Often people talk about the competencies required for the job. Sometimes "competency" is just another way of referring to the KSAOs needed for the job. Other times, "competency" means an aggregation of KSAOs. For example, interpersonal skills might be a competency that is composed of KSAOs such as listening skills, sensitivity to others, and assertiveness. Teamwork would be a competency composed of KSAOs such as conflict resolution skills, agreeableness, and oral communication skills. Occasionally, "competency" refers to the ability to perform some part of the job. So, the competency "relationship building" might point to a combination of tasks performed on a job and the KSAOs necessary to do those tasks. We have used both competency and KSAO throughout this book although we have tried to reserve KSAOs for talking about true knowledge, skills, abilities, and other characteristics and competencies for discussing larger groups of KSAOs.

Jobs Differ in Terms of the KSAOs Required

The trend toward organizational competency models suggests universal KSAO requirements or at least universal requirements within a given organization. Although some commonality of skill requirements exists across jobs at very general levels (e.g., many jobs require interpersonal skills, oral communication skills, and conscientiousness), most of these organizational competency models clearly acknowledge that jobs in the same organization require some specific KSAOs or different levels of the same competency that distinguish one job from another. For example, the kinds of interpersonal skills that a customer relations manager must have may be entirely different from the interpersonal skills required by an accounting manager. A financial analyst needs different kinds of reasoning skills from a cashier. If jobs did not differ, you could use a universal system of hiring for any job in the organization.

There is considerable research to suggest that *certain* KSAOs (e.g., cognitive ability or intellectual skills) have *some* relationship to successful performance in virtually any job; however, the relationship between cognitive ability and job performance is stronger in more complex jobs (2). Further, considerable research demonstrates that measurement of the other KSAOs in addition to cognitive ability increases the accuracy of the hiring systems. For example, the manager of IT infrastructure may need a great deal of cognitive ability, but the person who fills that job must also be extremely knowledgeable about network architecture. By measuring both sets of skills, the employer gets a more accurate prediction of future job success than measuring either alone.

Organizations Want to Hire Those Who Can Perform the Job Well

Organizations want to hire people who possess the KSAOs required to perform the job. The reasons for wanting capable employees are obvious. Those with the requisite skills perform at higher levels, and higher levels of performance can translate to higher productivity, larger profits, fewer errors, less waste, safer behavior, more training successes, less turnover, etc.

Organizations Want to Select the Best Individuals from a Given Applicant Pool

Most organizations want to hire the best candidates available to them. In general, if the job requires interpersonal skills, the person with better interpersonal skills is more desirable than the one with poorer interpersonal skills. Some organizations hire "top down," taking the best applicant first. Others define "best" by establishing the threshold level of skill required and treat all candidates who meet the standard as equally qualified. In some cases, more of the skill is not an asset. For example, an organization might require that all assembly line workers be able to lift and move objects weighing 10 pounds or less because the heaviest object on the assembly line weighs no more than 10 pounds. The ability to lift objects of greater weight is not important for this particular job. In other cases, the organization may define a level of a skill that is sufficient to do the job satisfactorily although more of the skill may be useful. For example, a company might set a standard for problem solving so that all service representatives in a call center who meet this standard can handle 80 percent of the problems presented in a reasonable period of time. However, people with higher levels of problem-solving skills may be able to handle more of the remaining 20 percent of the problems or deal with the 80 percent more quickly.

A few organizations do not bother with making an offer to the most highly qualified individuals, believing such applicants are unlikely to take the offer or will become bored quickly and leave the organization. However, this strategy of "take less than the best" generally occurs because the organization has not done a good job of specifying candidate requirements, recruiting the appropriate pool of candidates, or designing appropriate selection tools.

Organizations are Looking for an Efficient and Effective Process

Many a time have we heard "If I could just have someone do the job for a few months, I would know whether or not I should hire them." Performing the job is probably the most accurate test of all. Although you may gain better insight into an individual's KSAOs by observing actual job performance, there is a substantial trade-off between the costs of assessment and the benefits of accurate assessment. You can be super-thorough in assessment, but any process that requires too much candidate or hiring manager time and effort will not be efficient. Imagine the consequences of telling applicants that you will hire them, allowing them to perform the job for three months, then terminating those who fail to meet your performance standards! A few months on the job or even a three-day testing process will give you a fairly accurate reading of an individual's capabilities, but, for efficiency's sake, most organizations are more interested in balancing an "accurate enough" picture of an applicant with a process that is not unduly onerous and uses much shorter assessment tools.

The importance of the accuracy of the assessment depends upon the consequences of poor performance on the job. A fry cook lacking important KSAOs at a fast food restaurant may cause many problems ranging from long lines to undercooked burgers, but our fry cook is unlikely to cause too much damage to people or property. In contrast, an unqualified nuclear power plant operator could cause considerable damage.

People Differ in Whether They are Looking for Jobs, How They Hear about Jobs, and Whether They Actually Apply for Jobs

Sometimes organizations have a clear picture of what a job requires and how they should assess candidates' KSAOs, but their selection systems fall short in delivering high-quality candidates because they cannot find or attract candidates with the requisite skills. Selection and recruitment are very much intertwined – the "best" selection system will not be useful if you fail to attract good candidates, convince them to apply, or persuade them to accept the job offer.

Characteristics of "Good Selection Tools"

Before we discuss how to design a global selection system, we need to explain what makes for a good selection system anywhere. In the remainder of this chapter, we will cover the fundamentals for developing and implementing a high-quality hiring process. In Chapters 5 and 6, we will circle back to each of these fundamentals and discuss how they play out when considering a global selection system.

Good to Know

A good selection system . . .

- Is aligned with defined selection objectives
- Starts with gathering information about the job and the organizational context
- Involves careful development of each and every tool used
- Takes into account how information will be combined and integrated

- Is demonstrably effective
- Is not biased
- Is efficient
- Fits the staffing environment and uses staffing resources efficiently
- Can be marketed easily to key stakeholders
- Integrates the selection system with processes for monitoring implementation
- Is supported by effective recruitment practices

The table below provides a description of the most common types of selection tools – whether these are "good" for your particular context will be a function of the points we cover in the rest of this chapter.

Definitions:
Selection Tools

Cognitive ability tests measure mental abilities such as verbal or mathematical reasoning, reading comprehension, perceptual or analytic abilities. Cognitive abilities can be measured in a variety of ways; however, typically they are measured via written questions with multiple choice response options.

Structured interviews measure a wide variety of KSAOs using a standard set of questions and rating scales to evaluate the applicant. Structured interviews are almost always administered orally by an individual interviewer or a panel of interviewers, although occasionally we see a written interview administered via the Internet requiring written responses.

Unstructured interviews measure a variety of KSAOs using questions that vary from applicant to applicant and from interviewer to interviewer for the same job. Typically, the unstructured interview does not use rating scales for evaluations and is almost always administered orally. Although commonly used, unstructured interviews are not as good a predictor of job performance as structured interviews.

Work samples measure a variety of skills by having applicants perform tasks similar to those performed on the job. Typically, work samples use trained raters to evaluate performance and often provide checklists or behavioral anchors to define acceptable performance.

Job knowledge tests measure the knowledge required by a job. Often, a job knowledge test takes the form of a multiple choice test or an essay test, although sometimes we see oral tests that evaluate job knowledge. Work samples can also provide evidence of job knowledge.

Personality inventories measure a variety of traits related to job performance, turnover, and other outcomes of interest. Personality tests are often multiple choice instruments requiring the test taker to indicate the extent to which he/she agrees with a statement or the degree to which a statement represents his/her behavior.

Biographical information (some times called biodata) measures different KSAOs through questions about past experiences, education, and interests. Biodata are often collected through multiple choice tests although sometimes accomplishment records based on application data may be used.

Situational judgment tests measure a variety of KSAOs by presenting individuals with job-related scenarios (either in written or video form) and multiple responses to the situation, then asking for the most likely or most effective response, the best or the worst response, or the likelihood of doing each response.

Integrity tests measure attitudes and behavior regarding honesty, reliability, or acceptable behavior typically via multiple choice or true–false measures.

Assessment centers measure KSAOs through a series of work samples that are usually supplemented by any of the other predictors described above. Assessment centers typically involve multiple evaluators who synthesize information from all the tools used.

Reference checks gather information about past performance from those with previous experience with the individual.

Past education and experience measure KSAOs indirectly by inferring that people with certain education credentials or work experiences have certain KSAOs. For example, people with accounting degrees are believed to have knowledge of accounting principles.

Note: Table adapted from (3).

A Good Selection System is Aligned with Defined Selection Objectives

No undertaking will be successful if you don't define what you desire to achieve. Similarly, a selection system will not be successful if you don't invest time in identifying the specific objectives you want to accomplish before developing the general strategy for achieving them. Typically, this determination of a selection strategy begins with the organization's overall business objectives and business strategy, then drills down to the question, "What kinds of employees are necessary to fulfill the organization's goals?"

Once you have defined the objectives for your selection program, you might discuss the following questions in developing a strategy to achieve your goals:

What outcome(s) do you want to achieve?
This is a variant on the more general question of "How will we know if we are successful?" Most organizations would say the desired outcome is people who can do the job, which in turn relates to other desired outcomes such as greater productivity of the workforce, fewer errors or wastage, greater retention of employees, and attraction of higher-quality job candidates. Presumably, these outcomes translate into higher profits.

Are you selecting specialists or generalists?
You can hire individuals to fill specific, defined roles or hire individuals who have the potential to fill multiple roles as needed. For example, an organization may want to hire a compensation specialist who is expert in executive compensation or an HR generalist who can work effectively in staffing, compensation, labor relations, etc. For any given job category, your choice of generalist or specialist should depend on your assessments of future needs, the demands for certain skill sets in the organization, the degree of training needed to perform work, and the availability of specialists in the labor pool.

Are you selecting for an immediate contribution or for the potential to make a contribution?
Do you want someone who can "hit the ground running" or will you invest in training and developing a capable individual? This question

relates to the organization's approach to human capital. Is it "make or buy?" Is there an immediate need for certain skill sets? Can sufficient organizational resources be devoted to training and development for this position that hiring for future potential makes sense? If your organization does not focus on development for a given job, you need to acknowledge that to determine an appropriate hiring strategy.

Are you trying to address non-selection problems through your selection system (e.g., training, compensation, performance management)?
One scenario that repeats itself in many organizations is the hope that a new selection system will fix all employee problems. Unfortunately, no matter how good the selection system is, it cannot correct problems of poor supervision, inadequate training, lack of proper equipment, or inconsistent performance management. If your pay scale is below market levels or is applied inequitably, a new selection system will not make the job more attractive or reduce turnover problems. If your training is inadequate, a new selection system will not enhance performance levels. Your efforts at creating new selection systems should include an honest assessment of what problems need to be resolved and what the real causes are. Without a holistic assessment of the root causes of performance failures, even the best designed and implemented system will not help you achieve your objectives.

A Good Selection System Starts with Gathering Information about the Job and the Organizational Context

Successful problem solving starts with gathering the information needed to understand the problem(s) and to address the issues. In selection system design, there are at least three areas in which your information-gathering efforts should focus: the job, the hiring context, and the stakeholders. Figure 2.1 summarizes the information needs.

Job information
For selection system design, experts always advocate starting with a job analysis. A common mistake is assuming that a good understanding of a job exists because "we have a job description." Our Acme VP in our introductory example made the mistake of not gathering job

JOB INFORMATION	HIRING CONTEXT INFORMATION	VIEWS OF STAKEHOLDERS

• What work is performed
• Worker requirements /
  KSAOs
• Needed at entry or
  learned on the job
• Work setting description
	Labor Market
	• Employment rates
	• Trends in applicant pool
	  qualifications
	• Trends in applicant
	  mobility
	• Number of competitors
	• Salary and benefits
	  benchmarks
	• Competitor hiring practices
	
	Internal Staffing Context
	• Context of tool
	  administration
	• Nature of administrators
	• Options for system delivery
	• Technical and system
	  support needs
		Senior Leaders
		• Business objectives
		• Personnel needs
		• Desired outcomes/
		  expectations
		• Support for change
		
		Hiring Managers
		• Desired outcomes
		• Perceived challenges
		• Support for change
		• Labor market information
		• Profile of a successful
		  candidate
		
		HR Staff
		• Current system
		  effectiveness
		• Challenges to proposed
		  system
		• Obstacles to change
		• Support for change
		
		Applicants
		• Efficiency expectations
		• Fairness perceptions
		• Content expectations

Figure 2.1 Information Needs for a Global Selection System

information. He neglected the different kinds of sales positions (e.g., order taking, retail sales, and consultative sales) and ended up making some erroneous assumptions about similarities between jobs.

Best Practices and Common Pitfalls in Determining if Jobs are Similar

Best Practice
Take a detailed look at what the jobs involve, what tasks must be performed, what KSAOs are necessary to perform these tasks, and decide whether a common system can be used.

Common Pitfalls

- Job(s) with the same title in different locations are considered interchangeable when in fact they have different requirements.

- Job(s) with different titles are considered unique thus requiring separate systems when they are in essence similar in terms of skill requirements.
- Key job requirements are overlooked and not considered in selection.
- The minimum level of skill required is ignored.
- Requirements are put in place that are non-essential or that don't differentiate between good and poor performers.

Job analysis information can be collected in many ways, ranging from observations and interviews to job analysis questionnaires. It is beyond the scope of this book to discuss in detail all the possible approaches and their pros and cons. However, we can spell out a few basic "must do" practices (4).

Best Practices and Common Pitfalls in Job Analysis

Best Practices

- Systematically gather enough information to really understand the work performed regardless of where it is performed or by whom it is performed.
- Identify the worker requirements, including the levels of KSAOs needed to perform the job.
- Distinguish the KSAOs that are needed at entry into the job from those that can be learned on the job.
- Describe the setting in which the work is accomplished.

Common Pitfalls

- Outdated job descriptions remain in place.
- Revisions to job descriptions are made without any systematic data-gathering effort.
- Requirements are created based on what "would be nice" rather than what is actually required.

The level of detail required depends upon what information is already available and how the information will be used in support of a new selection system. For example, if existing information clearly establishes that knowledge of basic mechanical principles is needed for job performance, then little further detail may be needed. You may need very little job information to establish that coming to work and staying on the job is important. However, if the existing job information indicates the ability to manage conflict is important, and you want to develop interview questions and test questions that tap into the applicant's ability to handle the conflict situations faced on the job, more time must be spent gathering information about the types of conflict that occur and the appropriate responses given the organization's culture.

Hiring context information
A thorough understanding of the context in which hiring takes place is also necessary for success. There are two major components to the hiring context. The first involves the general labor market. In addition to general employment rates, you should gather information on trends in applicant pool qualifications (e.g., in the number of people obtaining a particular degree or credential, literacy rates), trends in applicant mobility (e.g., willingness to move to certain geographic locations), number of competitors in your location(s), and salary and benefits benchmarks (e.g., typical pay and benefits for a job). You might also engage in benchmarking competitor hiring practices (e.g., application process, time to hire, types of selection tools used, qualifications required), although we warn against viewing what everyone else is doing as the best way to achieve strategic goals.

The second component involves your internal staffing context. You need to understand how and when the selection system will be administered. For example, where does assessment occur? Who will handle each step of the hiring process? What are their capabilities? Do you expect applicants to come to your organization's locations or does applicant processing occur via the Internet, in an employment office, on a college campus, or some place else? What are the options for selection system delivery in your organization? Can technology be used? What are the limitations of technology? Is there technical support? If our Acme VP had taken the time to gather this type of information, some of his headaches might have been avoided.

Stakeholder perspectives information
Consultants on organizational change emphasize the importance of gathering support before embarking on any change initiative, and, of course, the same applies for selection system change. Selection system

change requires the support of many different stakeholder groups – having a senior-level organizational champion will not be sufficient to guarantee success. Some of the stakeholder perspectives you should gather early on in the process are:

- Views of senior leaders regarding business objectives, personnel needs, their desired outcomes of the new system, and their support for change. In exchange for their support, senior leaders need to know what it is realistic to expect and not to expect from a new selection system. In addition to the benefits of a good selection system, they must also be fully informed of the cost in terms of not only dollars paid for materials and consultants but also in terms of employee time in identifying job requirements and establishing the value of tools, setting standards, and so on.
- Views of hiring managers on desired outcomes, perceived challenges, and willingness to adopt new methods. Hiring managers also need to understand the costs and benefits of the new selection system. Knowing whether hiring managers have unrealistic expectations for a selection system change is just as critical as knowing the views of top management. Much of the employee time necessary to develop and validate good selection procedures will come from their budgets. Hiring managers can also provide information about the labor market, albeit shaded by their perspective. Finding out if hiring managers think the labor market is unfavorable or that applicants are receiving substantially larger offers from other firms is useful information, but it requires further verification. Perceptions are based on the experience of the individual hiring manager and may not reflect the broader picture, particularly when the goal is a global selection system. Finally, getting a read on the hiring manager's willingness to change the process and their objections to change will definitely be of value as you embark on development and implementation of a new system.

Because hiring managers must live with the results of a selection system, their views regarding a successful candidate are extremely important. Hiring managers usually know what tasks are performed by job incumbents and what level of skill is necessary for adequate performance. In addition, if hiring managers are involved in the selection process, they must understand both the cost and the value of their participation.

- Views of HR staff on current system effectiveness, new hiring practices, and obstacles to change. Those in HR involved in staffing are often the best repository of knowledge about what challenges the current system presents, how the hiring processes may change in the future, and what might be obstacles to change. Further, the HR staff is likely to play a key role in any system change, and their support for change efforts needs to be assessed.

  In most large organizations, HR is comprised of multiple functions whose employees may not share the same points of view regarding selection systems. For example, trainers may desire a selection system that produces quick learners of complex materials. In contrast, the recruiters who must fill positions may desire standards that are only high enough to ensure that new employees can perform minimally and that allow them to fill jobs quickly. Labor relations may want a hiring process that is highly proscribed and leaves little to the hiring manager's judgment to minimize grievances and other administrative challenges if the selection system is used for internal candidates. Consequently, it is important to capture all the relevant points of view in your planning.

- Views of applicants' expectations for the process. Job applicants have expectations regarding system efficiency (how quickly are job acceptance decisions made, how much time are they willing to devote to an application) and face-to-face interaction (how much, at what point in the process, with whom). In addition, applicants are often concerned about the fairness of the selection system and pay close attention to the content of selection tools and their job relevance. Applicants vary in their expectations. What works well for selecting hourly employees may be vastly different from what works for salaried professionals. Even among applicants for the same job, expectations will differ. Gathering information from applicants at an early stage can help you design a system which will have a high level of acceptability.

You probably cannot make everyone happy, and we are not advocating that you attempt to meet all the desires and expectations of various stakeholder groups. Indeed, the competing goals of stakeholders as well as the limited resources that can be devoted to a selection process can make it impossible to please everyone. Rather, we are suggesting you consider how you will respond to each stakeholder's needs and questions so you know what needs to be addressed throughout the change process, where misperceptions are likely to occur, what the likely sources of resistance are, and where you may need to really sell a particular option. Such information gathering would have alerted our Acme VP to some of the challenges he would be facing, making him better prepared to address them.

Case Scenario:
Incorporating Stakeholder Views

An examination of stakeholder views in a large manufacturer prior to design of a new global selection system for technical/production positions found important differences in perceptions of different kinds of selection tools (e.g., hiring managers felt tests were less fair than staffing and labor relations personnel) and criteria for system efficiency (e.g., HR personnel were more concerned and hiring managers less concerned with ease of use of tools). In selling the new system later, all internal stakeholders were presented with a matrix showing how the criteria they deemed important were met in the new system.

Source: (5).

A Good Selection System Involves Careful Development of Each and Every Tool Used

One of the more troubling situations we encounter is an organization that devotes considerable time, energy, and dollars into developing a "state-of-the-art" simulation using the latest technology but puts little or no thought into how other aspects of the selection process are developed. These organizations screen resumes and application information using no specified criteria or using criteria that are difficult to relate to the job. They sometimes provide no guidance to managers on how to develop and conduct interviews or allow managers to choose from the pool of test qualified applicants using personal criteria that are unrelated to the job and inconsistent across applicants. If you have developed or purchased a good measure of one job requirement yet left other important job requirements poorly screened, the goals of the selection system may not be fully met.

You can obtain carefully developed selection tools in several ways. You must decide if you will purchase selection tools that are off-the-shelf and ready-to-use, purchase off-the-shelf tools and customize them to your job and environment, or design and develop tools exclusively for your organization. Important considerations in making this decision include the expertise available to guide customization or development, the affordability of development, the tolerance of the time line for development, and the value of a unique selection system to your organization.

There are two critical steps to developing a selection system that you should make sure occur, regardless of whether you are designing a simple online application, a complex integrated video simulation, an interview, or any other form of testing; whether you are developing one selection tool or ten; whether the screening is for a low-level position or the CEO.

1 Choose the KSAOs on which you will screen based on solid information about the job
Understanding what is required to be successful in the job is the first step – typically a job analysis involves gathering information regarding the frequency with which certain tasks are performed and their importance and the importance of KSAOs necessary for accomplishing those tasks. This information may need further distillation: Which of these required KSAOs are covered during training and are not needed at the time of entry? Which ones are less important and therefore might be left out of a selection process for the sake of efficient process design? Which ones are truly critical differentiators between successful and unsuccessful performers? The result of this step should be a list of KSAOs that will be the focus of the selection process.

2 Determine what methods can best assess those KSAOs
As we noted in Chapter 1, a test can take many forms – one can assess interpersonal skills via an interview, a written test, a role-play simulation, biographical information, reference checking, or in some other way. Deciding which KSAOs will be assessed via what methods requires consideration of a host of factors: Which methods have been proven to be useful ways to assess a KSAO? What methods will work in your hiring context with your particular applicant population? What is the best trade-off between ensuring a thorough assessment of a KSAO (e.g., using multiple methods to assess)

and maximizing efficiency of the selection process (e.g., avoiding excessive redundancy in assessments)? What can you afford?

Gaining the answers to some of the questions posed here often requires relying on expert judgments, gathering information from researchers and vendors, and sifting and sorting lots of evidence. Ask experts for their views on each tool under review regarding these three key areas:

- *Psychometric considerations.* We will give a little more detail on this in the section on evaluating the effectiveness of a selection system, but essentially there are two questions of importance here:
  ◦ *How reliable is this component?* If you were to give someone this test or conduct this interview on Monday versus Friday, or if you asked Susan rather than Tom to score the assessment, you should come to the same conclusions regarding an applicant's skills and suitability for the job. An unreliable method is one on which a person's standing varies widely over time, place, or administrator.
  ◦ *What evidence supports the validity of inferences from this component?* If you are using an interview question to measure someone's conscientiousness, then you expect that the interview rating of that question is telling you something meaningful about that person's level of conscientiousness. If you are using a test score to predict future job performance, then you expect the test score tells you something about the likelihood of the test taker performing well on the job. Evidence of validity means that there is support for the accuracy of the conclusion you are reaching based on the results of the assessment. That is, if you conclude that Juan is conscientious based on a test score or interview rating, and Brad is not, those are correct conclusions.
- *Administration and scoring considerations.* What may be an ideal method for one job or one organization may not work well for another due to where, when, and how the selection system needs to be administered and scored. If hiring is done *en masse* once a year versus spread out over time, different methods might be more suitable for each hiring situation. If the locations for selection are public and not conducive for controlled assessment administration, paper-and-pencil tests requiring concentration may not be appropriate. If Internet access is limited or slow, Internet testing may need to be ruled out. If those who will be administering the component cannot be adequately trained or are not willing to take the

time to do so properly, then work simulations and structured interviews that require the interpretation of responses may not work. If employment decisions are made immediately after administration, then faxing answer sheets to a central location for scoring may not be feasible.

• *Acceptability.* We mentioned earlier the problems of stakeholder resistance. The information you gather on stakeholder views may play a role in determining which methods are likely to be implemented successfully. If hiring managers believe that the job is easily learned, they may resist the evaluation of cognitive skills. If the training organization is conscious of a limited training budget, they may not be happy with a selection system that focuses only on personal characteristics and ignores mental abilities. Applicants who must have graduate degrees to perform the job may be insulted if required to demonstrate their cognitive abilities or job knowledge even when there are vast differences in knowledge, skills, and abilities among those holding the degree.

To determine what methods will be used to measure each of the KSAOs, a KSAO by method matrix should be created (see box for example) to ensure that all KSAOs are adequately covered and that all aspects of the selection process are truly necessary. The need for redundancy of measures is a matter of professional judgment. For example, including a complex simulation to tap one particular skill (e.g., leadership) may be unnecessary if leadership is already adequately assessed via a scored biographical instrument and an interview, or leadership may be deemed so important as to warrant the most thorough examination possible.

A Good Selection System Takes into Account How Information will be Combined and Integrated

Selection systems can be comprised of a single tool (e.g., a structured interview) or multiple tools (e.g., tests, interviews, background screens, work samples). Any system with multiple components must define how the various parts will be integrated so that one decision about hiring can be made. (Similar decisions must be made when there are multiple parts in one tool (e.g., scores for several KSAOs in

Example: **KSAO Method Matrix**				

KSAO	**Cognitive Test**	**Call Simulation**	**Interview**	**Reference Check**
Oral communi-cation		x	x	x
Ability to learn new product infor-mation	x			x
Ability to adapt to changing customer needs	x	x	x	x
Emotional stability/ ability to handle irate customers		x	x	x

a structured interview; quantitative and verbal scores on tests of cognitive ability)). There are three decisions that are explicitly or implicitly made with regard to integrating information:

1 Will you have multiple hurdles or a compensatory scoring?
One choice point is whether to use a multiple hurdle or compensatory model for the process. Figure 2.2 provides an illustration of these models. Multiple hurdle models require the candidate to qualify on each component of the selection system. (See Figure 2.2a.) For

(a)

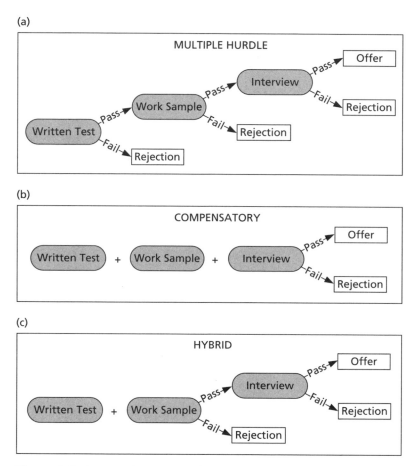

Figure 2.2 Approaches to Combining Tests

example, all qualified candidates must pass a cognitive ability test and an interview. Sometimes all components are administered simultaneously, and the candidate must pass each (e.g., a candidate must have a passing score on the cognitive ability test and the structured interview). Other times, the candidate must pass one component before proceeding to the next (e.g., only those passing the verbal test are invited to take the math test; 6).

A compensatory model requires a candidate to meet a total qualifying score across all tools. (See Figure 2.2b.) For example, the cognitive ability test score and interview scores are combined to create a total score. Thus, a lower score on the cognitive ability test can be compensated for by higher scores on the interview. Sometimes, compensatory models are used within a tool. For example, a test that has verbal and quantitative items may be scored such that there is one total score, and high skill levels in one area will compensate for poorer skills in the other.

A third model is a hybrid model that combines the multiple hurdles model and the compensatory model. (See Figure 2.2c.) An interview score and a test score may be combined in a total score used to determine overall qualification status; however, a candidate may be required to earn a minimum score on each dimension of the interview that is scored.

This decision regarding the appropriate model should be based primarily on the extent to which the KSAOs measured by each instrument are truly compensatory and a minimum level of the KSAO is necessary to perform the job. For example, an accounting job might require both conscientiousness and math abilities; however, high conscientiousness does not compensate for poor math skills, and the accounting job requires high levels of both.

Often in practice, administrative considerations (e.g., the ease of administering multiple tools at once and the costs of doing so) influence the choice of model. In competitive labor markets, an employer may be reluctant to ask the candidate to come back multiple times, so all tools are administered at the same time. (Sometimes in such cases, the tools are still scored using multiple hurdles.) When one selection tool is very expensive to administer (e.g., face-to-face interview, work simulation), an employer may find it more cost effective to administer the interview only to those who have passed earlier, less expensive screens.

The model for combining scores across instruments also applies to combining scores within a single instrument that measures multiple KSAOs. For example, an interview may cover six areas important to job performance. An average of ratings of the six areas implies a compensatory belief about these six areas. So strong leadership skills could make up for weaker job knowledge. In contrast, requiring a minimum level of certain skills such as job knowledge creates a hurdle each applicant has to meet.

2 What is the optimal sequencing of components?

Another consideration, regardless of whether each method is being used as a hurdle or integrated into a compensatory score, is the optimal order of administering components. Decisions on order are often based on ideas about what constitutes the most efficient staffing flow. Sometimes, the most efficient process is to administer each component in a separate session; sometimes all together. Even if two components are used as separate hurdles (e.g., a passing score on a measure of cognitive ability and a passing score on a measure of conscientiousness), it may be administratively more efficient to administer them in one testing session.

Many organizations choose to use the tool that is either the least expensive or the easiest to administer first, followed by the more expensive and harder to administer instrument. So, an unproctored biodata survey administered over the Internet may precede a structured interview that is administered face-to-face. Our Global VP at Acme faced some sequencing questions related to the efficiency and feasibility of administering the components of his selection system. In the USA, some organizations order their selection tools in hopes of enhancing the demographic diversity of their final set of selected candidates. Occasionally, organizations put their least onerous selection procedure first to prevent applicants from dropping out of the hiring process prematurely.

3 Should you use any "prescreening"?

In the Internet Age, many job openings are widely posted, and individuals can easily apply for jobs for which they are not even remotely qualified because the effort required for application is quite low (e.g., email a resume). Further, in certain job markets with high unemployment or for certain very attractive jobs (e.g., those that pay well and/or provide extraordinary benefits), unqualified individuals may apply with the outside hope of securing a plum job. In these cases, you might employ simple prescreening devices – such as brief phone screens or online assessments that ask a series of simple yes/no questions to determine applicant eligibility – to quickly remove the grossly unqualified from the applicant pool. Eligible applicants are then directed to the remainder of the selection process.

Example:
Sequencing

Suppose you have 100 applicants and are administering a personality test, a work sample demonstrating the ability to use spreadsheets, and a one-hour interview. The personality test costs $20.00 to administer and score. Because of the need for an expert to evaluate performance on the work sample, it costs $50 to administer and score. The interview costs $20 to administer and evaluate. Here are several possible sequences, given a 50 percent pass rate on each:

Sequence 1:

- Give 100 personality tests ($2,000); 50 percent pass so then give 50 work samples ($2,500); 50 percent pass so conduct 25 interviews ($500) = total cost of $5,000

Sequence 2:

- Give 100 work samples ($5,000); 50 percent pass so then give 50 personality tests ($1,000); 50 percent pass so conduct 25 interviews ($500) = total of $6,500

Sequence 3:

- Give 100 candidates all three tests: 100 personality tests ($2,000); 100 work samples ($5,000); 100 interviews ($2,000) = total $9,000

Different pass rates might make one rethink which sequencing is better.

Sequence 1:

- Give 100 personality tests ($2,000); 90 percent pass rate so then give 90 work samples ($4,500); 50 percent pass rate so conduct 45 interviews ($900) = total of $7,400

Sequence 2:

- Give 100 work samples ($5,000); 50 percent pass so then give 50 personality tests ($1,000); 90 percent pass rate so conduct 45 interviews ($900) = total of $6,900

Sequence 3:

- Give 100 candidates all three tests: 100 personality tests ($2,000); 100 work samples ($5,000); 100 interviews ($2,000) = total $9,000

Example:
Prescreening Questions

- Do you have a reliable means of transportation to our work location?
- Are you legally able to work in this country?
- Are you available to work evening and weekend shifts?
- Are you willing to work outdoors in cold or wet weather?
- Do you have a state license to practice nursing?

If these questions are job-relevant, answering no to any of the questions would make the individual ineligible for further consideration.

Some organizations develop minimum qualifications for jobs and use them to screen out the unqualified. Minimum qualifications often consist of education and experience requirements. For example, a middle management engineering job whose incumbent will manage bridge construction might require a four-year degree in Engineering, a Professional Engineer license, and ten years of project management experience related to bridge building. It is important to note that both prescreen questions and minimum qualifications are tests and should be job-related.

A Good Selection System's Effectiveness is Supported by Data

We mentioned earlier the notion that choosing a selection method involves considering the strength of the evidence supporting the validity of the method (or the accuracy of the inferences made from the score). You need to know whether the method you choose will give you the results you desire. When developing a new method or customizing a method to your organization, evidence regarding the usefulness of the selection method in your situation may be unavailable. A plan for gathering such information on selection component effectiveness is essential.

There are whole books on validating selection processes, and the validation of a selection instrument that meets professional and legal standards typically requires a trained professional. We will not reiterate their contents here; however, to give you a sense of what types of information you may want to gather in support of your selection process, the table below provides examples of different types of validity evidence that might be gathered, either prior to implementing a new process (ideally) or after the process has been implemented.

Examples: Validity Evidence	
Sources of validity evidence (4)	**Examples**
Does the candidate's score on the assessment method relate to work-relevant behavior or work outcomes? When the criterion for evaluating the effectiveness of a test is job performance, validity evidence can be gathered by testing job applicants and waiting a period of time after hire to gather performance information or by testing employees and evaluating their current work performance.	• Those who are rated highly in the interview perform better on the job than those with lower ratings. • Those who score high on a biographical inventory are less likely to turnover quickly than those who score lower.
Does the candidate's score on the assessment method relate to scores on other measures of the same thing?	• Those who score high on a situational judgment test of leadership also get high ratings by interviewers on the dimension of leadership. • Individuals who score high on a new test of extraversion also score high on an older, established measure of extraversion.

Continued

Sources of validity evidence (4)	Examples
Does the content of the assessment match the content of the job?	• Job applicants are asked to perform a task in a work sample very similar to the task they would do regularly on the job. • An interview question asks about a common customer situation found on the job.
Does the internal structure of the assessment support that it measures what is intended?	• A test claims to measure three types of conflict management skills and when the data are appropriately analyzed, three dimensions emerge.
Have researchers accumulated enough evidence from previous uses of the tool to justify its use?	• Researchers examine whether a biographical inventory relates to turnover in a number of separate studies for different types of sales jobs and then quantitatively synthesize this information to conclude that this tool relates to turnover for all sales jobs.

When developing and validating employment tools, most professionals focus on two forms of validity evidence: (i) demonstrating the relationship between scores and the criterion of interest (e.g., job performance); or (ii) demonstrating the relationship between the content of the tool and the content of the job. Sometimes, you will see these validation strategies referred to as "criterion-related validity" and "content-related validity" strategies respectively.

Although you will want to know how well a specific assessment works for your job in your environment, considerable research already exists on common selection methods. Many professionals use the research literature to choose selection instruments that are most likely to be effective and then conduct a local study to evaluate their effectiveness for a specific job in a particular environment where needed. The table overleaf (3) provides a summary of some common selection methods that have been shown to be effective (i.e., related to job performance) across jobs. The values in the column labeled "validity" reflect relationships between scores on the tool and job performance and range from −1.0 to 1.0. A 1.0 indicates perfect correspondence between tool scores and performance scores. The higher the number is, the stronger the relationship between selection tool score and performance. A 0.0 indicates there is no relationship between the tool and job performance; a −1.0 indicates a perfect, inverse relationship.

The information in the table reflects potential validity values rather than the actual values found in any given operational setting. The specific validity coefficient you obtain for your selection process will depend on how well developed the specific tool you use is, which tools are used in combination, how carefully your work outcome measure is developed and collected, what the characteristics of your study sample are, how you design your study, and other operational factors.

In addition to validity evidence, costs are often an important consideration in the choice of selection method. The table also includes a high-level evaluation of the costs to develop the tools and the costs to administer them. Note that within each category of selection method there is considerable variability in the costs, and your actual costs may differ from these estimates considerably.

While some of these tools may be better predictors than others and some may be less expensive than others, what you include in your selection process will depend on what KSAOs your job analysis supports, what is operationally feasible in your staffing environment, and what other strategic goals are important.

Validation evidence showing the selection method effectively identifies capable employees and development and delivery costs are important but not the only aspects related to showing that a selection system is effective. In addition, most employers consider the following:

Good to Know

Tool	Validity	Costs (development/ administration)
Cognitive ability tests	.51	Low/low
Structured interviews	.51	High/high
Unstructured interviews	.31	Low/high
Work samples	.54	High/high
Job knowledge tests	.48	High/low
Conscientiousness	.31	Low/low
Biographical information	.35	High/low
Situational judgment tests	.34	High/low
Integrity tests	.41	Low/low
Assessment centers	.37	High/high
Reference checks	.26	Low/low

Note: Table adapted from (3). Sources of validity coefficients: (2, 7). Values are derived from meta-analyses and have been adjusted for many of the common sources of error in validation studies. Labels high and low are relative to other tools rather than based on a specific cost level.

- Compliance with legal standards
- Consideration of diversity goals
- Stakeholder acceptance

Legal standards, attitudes toward diversity, and diversity goals are often determined by national laws and culture, topics we will cover in Chapters 3 and 4. Stakeholder acceptance is a topic we will address shortly.

A Good Selection System is Not Biased

Good selection systems evaluate KSAOs without regard to irrelevant personal characteristics. Moreover, applicants want to be treated fairly and not penalized in employment situations by their race, sex, national origin, or other irrelevant personal characteristics. Establishing fairness or lack of bias requires research, which is beyond the scope of this book, to answer the key question: *Is the assessment method free from bias or contamination that negatively affects the scores of some?* To show a lack of bias, you might provide evidence that interviewer ratings predicted rates of turnover in the same way for males and females. Note that we did not say that males and females have the same scores on the interview. Rather, an unbiased tool predicts the work outcome of interest in the same way for both groups.

Evidence of bias may require that you change selection tools or the way in which they are used. In an interview, you might need to train interviewers to be careful about rating women differently from men simply because they are women. Similarly, you might use a math word problems test for selection into a job that does not require facility in the English language. However, you may find that native English-language speakers who score poorly on a test do not do well on the job but non-native English-language speakers who score poorly on the test sometimes do well on the job. Consequently, you might need to consider translating the test into other languages (assuming speaking English on the job is not required), clarifying the instructions on the test, or conducting research to revise the test.

A Good Selection System Meets Efficiency Requirements

A well-designed selection system could meet all the requirements noted above, but still not be implemented or used for long. A key to success is also meeting the efficiency requirements of the organization. These include considerations of cost, time, technology, and labor market. (See Figure 2.3.)

Cost

As noted in the table presented earlier, the costs of developing and administering a selection system vary. Methods such as interviews

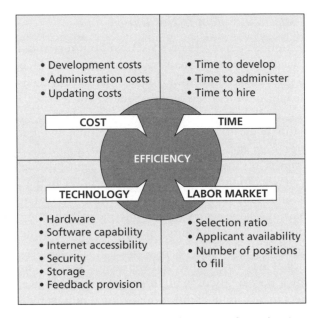

Figure 2.3 Factors Affecting the Efficiency of a Selection System

can be relatively easy to develop and validate using a content-oriented strategy compared to situational judgment tests (SJTs) that require a lengthy development process, or personality measures that require complex validation work based on criterion-oriented strategies. Selection instruments that require one-on-one administration (e.g., interviews, work samples, role plays) usually cost more than instruments that can be administered to larger groups of people at one time by one administrator or that can be computer-administered. Although some selection tools (e.g., arithmetic tests) need few revisions over time, others require more maintenance. Selection programs including a structured interview often need constant interviewer training and calibration to ensure the interviews are conducted properly. The effectiveness of work samples is dependent upon a cadre of well-trained administrators and scorers. Video-based SJTs can become outdated as quickly as fashion and hairstyles change. The costs of updates need to be planned to prevent a quick obsolescence.

Time

Time is an important yardstick for measuring system efficiency. First, you should consider how long it will take to develop and launch a new system and determine whether the organization can afford that length of time. If you need the system yesterday, you may not be able to wait a year for a test to be developed for you. Off-the-shelf products usually do not have the same time-to-develop issues as customized measures, but they may be less suitable or less effective in your environment. If the need for the new selection system is critical, the time to develop may lead you to choose a less time-consuming option. However, we need to note that as with many other things in life, investing time in development rather than taking shortcuts pays in the long run.

The time taken to administer the process can be an important concern too. Although there is little systematic evidence collected, many staffing personnel believe that applicants are highly sensitive to the amount of time spent testing – particularly if the tests are administered via the Internet in unproctored settings. In addition, HR staff and hiring managers are often conscious of their staffing goals related to cost and time to fill requisitions. Further, the time of system administrators (e.g., interviewers, assessment raters) is also crucial as their time directly relates to costs. However, we need to note that shaving three minutes from the time spent assessing the candidates but reducing reliability and validity in doing so can lead to a minimally more efficient process with a dramatic drop in effectiveness.

Finally, another time consideration is the amount of time from the submission of an application to the placement of a qualified new hire. Selection systems containing multiple hurdles that require an applicant to return to the employer on several separate occasions may lengthen the time needed in the hiring process. Information gathered during the context and stakeholder analyses mentioned previously will give you a picture of what a tolerable limit is for the time-to-hire in your organization.

Technology

The technology needs of a hiring system have become an increasingly important consideration in planning selection systems. Both hardware and test administration software have improved rapidly, making computerized testing and Internet-based testing feasible and affordable in many situations. However, there are many questions remaining that must be addressed before you embark on computerized assessments.

Example:
Questions to Ask Regarding Technology

- Is technology available in all locations where you will hire?
- Is there a reliable power supply for the technology?
- Do you have sufficient computers in hiring centers for applicants to use?
- If the tool is Internet-based, do applicants have reliable Internet access?
- Can your test administration platform administer the type of question you plan to use?
- Can your test administration platform combine scores in the ways you plan?
- Do you have technology that can ensure the security of materials and applicant information?
- Does computerized assessment require skills that are not required on the job?
- What screen resolution or access speed is necessary for this selection assessment to be viewed properly by all applicants?
- What candidate information should be stored centrally versus locally?
- Is instantaneous feedback going to be provided, and, if so, do you have the capacity to provide it?
- What concerns regarding privacy and security of personal information arise when transmitting information?
- What safeguards regarding security of materials need to be in place?

If our Global VP of Sales at Acme had paused to ask these questions before his global roll-out, think of all the hassles he would have avoided!

Labor market
Labor market conditions affect system efficiency. The selection ratio is the number of individuals hired relative to the number who apply. Ideally, the recruiting effort ensures sufficient numbers of candidates

to make good decisions. Selection implies that there are choices to make. If you have only a few applicants, a selection system may not be as useful as when you have many – you have to take them all just to fill your positions. If almost everyone passes or almost everyone fails, the system may not be very helpful. If everyone passes and you have a small number of openings, you still don't have a tool to guide your choice. If no one passes and you have many openings, there is no one to choose. Keep in mind too that some recruiting processes are expensive propositions, and generating an excessive number of candidates can be costly. Ideally, your recruiting process produces enough qualified people so that you can fill your positions even when declinations are factored into your headcount.

A Good Selection System fits the Staffing Environment and Uses Staffing Resources Efficiently

A good selection system can be managed by the people who must use it (8). That is, the system can be administered in the setting and by the staff available without compromising its effectiveness. A test of reasoning should not be administered in a noisy place that allows the test taker to be interrupted. A computerized test can't be administered by people who don't understand the test administration software. A work sample on electric wiring can't be scored unless there is someone who understands the wiring required in the sample.

Tips:
Matching Selection System with Environment

- Interviewers, test administrators, and scorers are available.
- Interviewers, test administrators, and scorers have the necessary skills and are appropriately trained.
- The technology to administer the system is available, reliable, and sufficiently familiar to those who will use it (administrators as well as applicants).
- The environment for administering the selection tools is appropriate (e.g., not too noisy for testing, private when necessary).

A Good Selection System is Supported by Appropriate Policies and Procedures

The staffing environment should have in place policies and procedures that protect the company's investment in materials and ensures fair and equitable treatment of all applicants for a job.

Policies regarding retesting, exemptions, confidentiality, test security, and cheating should be developed and communicated prior to system implementation. It is surprising that so much time and money may be put into developing a system with no thought given to how the organization will respond to these questions. Answers to these questions may require input from many stakeholders as well as a process to work out differences of opinion. Managers often feel that the great intern who worked with them last summer should be exempt from the testing requirement or that an individual who doesn't pass a test should be allowed to try again the next day. To ensure that everyone is treated fairly, policies for exceptions to normal practice must be defined and applied consistently.

Selection system materials must be secure. Again, it is surprising and most disheartening to see an organization invest heavily in developing a new selection tool that is quickly compromised. When candidates know "the right answers," the assessment is not valid and prediction of any job outcome will be inaccurate. There are many ways to allow a tool to be compromised, ranging from lax storage and document handling procedures to weak proctoring practices that allow individuals to take questions. Although most people would agree that individuals should be hired based on their merits, organizations are often lax about ensuring that assessment materials are kept secure.

A Good Selection System can be Marketed Easily to Key Stakeholders

To win acceptance of your selection system, you must market its value to many stakeholders. Most marketing strategies try to convince all stakeholders that the tool measures important components of the job. Face validity (i.e., the extent to which the selection tool appears to measure important job requirements) helps stakeholders see the relationship between the tool and job performance. Research evidence that supports system effectiveness is only useful if you can translate it into terms that are understandable to your stakeholders and convince them that the system will deliver desirable employees. A bit of planning in this regard would have made our Acme VP's life so much simpler.

Another important stakeholder group is the applicants themselves. In addition to face validity, most applicants want to understand what is expected of them in the selection process. Appropriate orientation materials can help make applicants aware of what the selection process will entail, how decisions will be made, and how they can prepare. Considerable research has shown that beliefs that the process is ethical, accurate, unbiased, and consistent across all applicants lead to perceptions that the system is fair (9). Also, feelings that one is informed about the bases for decision-making, has input into the process, and has opportunities for appeal or correction of errors also influence perceptions of fairness (9). Orientation can be as simple as including information in the instructions for an application or test or as elaborate as question and answer sessions hosted by the organization specifically for applicants.

A Good Selection System is One in which Systems for Monitoring Implementation are in Place

In the Information Age, a growing challenge is ensuring that the right information is collected and accessible to the people who need it (and not accessible to those who have no need to know). With selection systems, not only do hiring managers and HR departments need accurate information on applicants and on the hiring process, but those responsible for selection systems also need to monitor certain types of information to assess matters such as the current effectiveness of the selection system, the need for system change, trends in the applicant population, and so on. For example, test score increases may signal that a test has been compromised in some way; conversely, a decrease in test scores may suggest that the applicant pool has changed in substantive ways. Some organizations are notorious for investing in selection system design only to do such a poor job of tracking the outcomes of the system that they are unable to judge whether it is truly producing the type of employees desired. Planning for monitoring needs to occur before, not after, implementation.

A Good Selection System is Supported by Effective Recruitment Practices

We noted at the beginning of this chapter that selection and recruitment are intertwined. As noted in our discussion of selection ratios, there needs to be a sufficient flow of capable applicants into the system for a selection process to achieve its potential.

Best Practices and Common Pitfalls in Recruitment

Best Practices

- Identify capable candidates in sufficient numbers.
- Allow for effective self-selection.
- Generate the interest of capable applicants, attract them, maintain their interest in the company, and lead to offer acceptance.

Common Pitfalls

- Failure to give attention to generating enough interest in the job.
- Failure to give sustained attention to the candidate to keep them engaged in the hiring process.
- Failure to give sufficient information to applicants, preventing them from making good decisions about fit with the job.

In an effective recruitment process, candidates should feel the process is informative (i.e., they get the information they want about the organization and the job) and that their personal treatment has been positive.

More and more organizations are recognizing that it is to the benefit of both the candidate and the organization to provide some upfront guidance to potential applicants regarding their job suitability. By providing information about the job and its requirements, organizations expect an unqualified individual will not waste the organization's (or their own) time and resources by pursuing a job with little hope of success. The methods by which you can encourage self-selection vary, but some common methods are noted in the box below.

Best Practices and Common Pitfalls in Encouraging Self-Selection

Best Practices

- Providing a sufficiently detailed job description so applicants can judge their qualifications and interest appropriately.
- Providing a "realistic job preview" highlighting job requirements and working conditions, particularly those that applicants may be unaware of or overlook (e.g., standing all day, dealing with impatient customers).
- Providing a tool for assessing fit. These range from a simple set of questions ("Do you like working with animals?") to scored tools regarding values and interests.

Common Pitfalls

- Hoping candidates will find accurate information about your company.
- Ignoring candidates' needs for information.
- Focusing too heavily on "selling" the job and glossing over features that might be less desirable.

Example:
Realistic Job Previews (RJP)

Many organizations have RJPs on their websites to help potential applicants decide whether a job is right for them. For example, to give a candidate a feel for what the job would be like on a day-to-day basis, Wachovia provides web-based videos for some of its job families that provide a job overview and sample customer interactions (10). Similarly, Barclays Bank in Great Britain provides information about each business and career profiles that describe jobs and what real people like about their work (11). BMW offers virtual plant tours on its website (12). Some organizations use RJPs for jobs for which many applicants have unrealistic

Continued

expectations. For example, the Idaho State Police website notes that the job of a trooper is different than what is depicted on television or in the movies and provides potential candidates with a clear list of what the typical job duties are (13). Other organizations use RJPs to highlight job aspects that may not be apparent to most potential applicants and may be undesirable. For example, Bruce Power provides an RJP for nuclear power plant operators that emphasizes the number of repetitive tasks (14). Even organizations that struggle to find good applicants use RJPs to provide a balanced picture of the advantages and disadvantages of the job. For example, Dungarvin provides an RJP for direct support professionals who will be working with individuals with mental and physical disabilities, so they are aware of the types of assistance they might provide (bathing, dressing, eating) and the challenging client behaviors they might encounter (verbal abuse, hitting) as well as the many positive aspects of direct support work (15).

Think about it!

❖ What are your assumptions regarding selection systems? Are they acknowledged and shared? Are they realistic?

❖ What is your selection strategy? What do you wish to predict? Are you selecting specialists or generalists? Are you selecting for immediate contribution or potential? Are you making or buying your selection tools? Are you trying to address non-selection problems through your selection system?

❖ What indicators of effectiveness should you track in order to judge success in meeting your specific objectives?

❖ Have you gathered sufficient information on the job, the hiring context, and the views of stakeholders to lay the groundwork for your system?

❖ For job information, have you described the work performed, identified work requirements, distinguished what is needed at entry from what is needed on the job, and described the work setting?

❖ For hiring context information, have you monitored the labor market, noted trends in applicant qualifications and mobility, benchmarked on competitor offers and hiring practices, and clarified your IT and physical constraints for selection system delivery?

❖ For stakeholder perspectives, have you consulted with senior leaders, hiring managers, HR and applicants? Do you know what expectations these groups have and what challenges they foresee?

❖ Have you based your choice of KSAOs to screen on using solid job information?

❖ In determining what methods to use, have you taken into account psychometric qualities of tools, administration and scoring concerns, and acceptability to stakeholders?

❖ Have you developed a KSA/tool matrix to provide overall guidance?

❖ Are your decisions regarding compensatory combination or multiple hurdles logically justified? Cost justified?

❖ Have you considered whether prescreening may be helpful?

❖ Do the tools you are considering have sufficient validity evidence to support their effectiveness in your context or are you willing to collect such evidence?

❖ Are the selection procedures job-related?

❖ Are you providing applicants with information they need to self-select appropriately?

❖ Have you evaluated (or do you plan to evaluate) the process for bias?

❖ Can the selection tools be properly administered in the staffing environment that exists?

❖ Have you developed policies regarding retesting, exemptions, confidentiality and cheating and do you communicate and enforce these policies?

❖ Do you have a plan for marketing the system to internal stakeholders?

❖ Have you considered what orientation to provide applicants and how it will be delivered?

❖ Have you considered what types of information you would like to monitor after implementation and have you designed mechanisms for doing so?

❖ Do applicants see your process as informative?

❖ Are those involved in the hiring process trained/selected to be warm, friendly, and interpersonally engaging?

❖ Does the system meet your requirements for efficiency in terms of time and cost?

❖ Have you considered your technological capacities and factored in any technology costs?

❖ Do you have a low selection ratio (i.e., many applicants for few positions)? What steps might you take to get your current selection ratio lower?

References for Chapter 2

1 Guion, 1998.
2 Schmidt & Hunter, 1998.
3 Ryan & Tippins, 2003.
4 Society for Industrial and Organizational Psychology, 2003.
5 Ryan, Hemingway, Carr, & Highhouse, unpublished.
6 Tippins, 2002.
7 McDaniel, Morgeson, Finnegan, Campion, & Braverman, 2001.
8 Higgs, Papper, & Carr, 2000.
9 Leventhal, 1980.
10 http://www.wachovia.com/inside/page/0,,137_371_372_374,00.html. Downloaded 2/27/08.
11 http://www.personal.barclays.co.uk/BRC1/jsp/brcontrol?task=articleFW about&site=pfs&value=13465&menu=5500. Downloaded 2/27/08.
12 http://www.bmwusfactory.com/build/. Downloaded 2/27/08.
13 http://www.isp.state.id.us/hr/trooper_info/realistic_job.html.Downloaded 2/27/08.
14 http://www.brucepower.com/uc/GetDocument.aspx?docid=2288. Downloaded 2/27/08.
15 http://www.dungarvin.com/Employment/Realistic%20Job%20Preview/RJP-page01.htm. Downloaded 2/27/08.

Suggestions for Further Reading

Brannick, M. T., & Levine, E. L. (2002). *Job analysis: Methods, research, and applications for human resource management in the new millennium.* Thousand Oaks, CA: Sage.

Chapter 3

Cultural Differences and Their Impact on Selection Systems

You may be concerned about how cultural differences between countries will affect your ability to come up with a common selection system. After all, there are clearly differences in cultures around the globe and there are also significant differences in how selection is carried out around the world.

Examples
• In Japan, vague job descriptions are not viewed negatively as they are felt to inspire more commitment and responsibility than a limiting job description (1).
• In China, personality traits are considered more important than skills and abilities in hiring decisions (2).
• Indians have a very lax view of privacy and will not hesitate to ask very personal questions in hiring contexts; Chinese do not have the same sense of privacy as Americans and would expect others to talk about age, family, and money (3).

In Chapter 1, we mentioned a 20-country study that indicated differences in which tools tend to be used in different locations. The table below summarizes differences for managerial jobs. While the table indicates *average* levels of use, there was a great deal of variability within countries in the use of different methods. Further, when one considers non-managerial jobs, there is even greater variability across organizations within a given country (4). Also, many countries were not represented in this study. Nevertheless, there appears to be some patterns in types of selection instruments preferred in various countries.

Use of Selection Tools[a,b]

Tool	Rarely Used on Average
Cognitive Ability Test	Australia, France, Germany, Hong Kong, Italy, Japan, Malaysia
Foreign Language Test	Australia, Canada, Germany, Ireland, Italy, Japan, Malaysia, Netherlands, New Zealand, Portugal, Singapore, South Africa, Sweden, United Kingdom, USA
Personality Tests	Germany, Italy, Japan, Malaysia, USA
Simulation Exercise	Australia, France, Germany, Greece, Hong Kong, Ireland, Italy, Japan, Malaysia, New Zealand, Singapore, Spain, Sweden, USA
Application Form	Sweden
Educational Qualifications	Spain
Employer References	Germany, Greece, Spain
One-to-one Interviews	
Panel Interviews	France, Germany, Italy, Spain
Biodata	Australia, Belgium, Canada, France, Hong Kong, Ireland, Italy, Japan, Malaysia, Netherlands, New Zealand, Portugal, Singapore, South Africa, Spain, Sweden, United Kingdom, USA

Notes: [a]Table adapted from (4). [b]Integrity Tests and Situational Judgment Tests were rarely used in any country. Interest Inventories were rarely used in any country – with the exception of Portugal, where their use was occasional.

Occasional Use on Average	*Frequent Use on Average*
Canada, Greece, Ireland, New Zealand, Portugal, Singapore, South Africa, Sweden, United Kingdom, USA	Belgium, Netherlands, Spain
Belgium, France, Greece, Hong Kong, Spain	
Australia, Canada, France, Greece, Hong Kong, Ireland, Netherlands, Portugal, Singapore, United Kingdom	Belgium, New Zealand, South Africa, Spain, Sweden
Belgium, Canada, Netherlands, Portugal, South Africa, United Kingdom	
Canada, Greece, Ireland, Portugal, Spain	Australia, Belgium, France, Germany, Hong Kong, Italy, Japan, Malaysia, Netherlands, New Zealand, Singapore, South Africa, United Kingdom, USA
Belgium	Australia, Canada, France, Germany, Greece, Hong Kong, Ireland, Italy, Japan, Malaysia, Netherlands, New Zealand, Portugal, Singapore, South Africa, Sweden, United Kingdom, USA
Belgium, France, Italy, Japan, Netherlands, Portugal, Singapore	Australia, Canada, Hong Kong, Ireland, Malaysia, New Zealand, South Africa, Sweden, United Kingdom, USA
Hong Kong, Ireland	Australia, Belgium, Canada, France, Germany, Greece, Italy, Japan, Malaysia, Netherlands, New Zealand, Portugal, Singapore, South Africa, Spain, Sweden, United Kingdom, USA
Belgium, Greece, Portugal, Singapore, Sweden, USA	Australia, Canada, Hong Kong, Ireland, Japan, Malaysia, Netherlands, New Zealand, South Africa, United Kingdom
Germany	Greece

The differences in approaches to selection in locations around the world beg the question of how these variations will affect your ability to achieve a global selection system. We discuss some of the factors that lead to these differences – legal, economic, educational – in the next chapter. Here we focus on how culture influences selection practices and how culture should be taken into account in the design of selection systems. That is, knowing what the cultural differences are and how they influence individuals' beliefs and behaviors can help you to develop a system that gains global acceptance from hiring managers and applicants.

What is Culture?

The word "culture" is one that most people assume they understand; yet in practice, it is used to refer to many different things. At its core, "culture" connotes stable characteristics of a group that differentiate it from other groups. It often refers to shared values, beliefs, and interpretations of events that arise from the common experiences of members of a group (5). The "group" can be defined in many different ways. In this chapter, the group of interest is based on nationality (e.g., German) or geographic region (e.g., Asia), but we can also talk about the culture of a corporation (e.g., P&G has a strong culture), the culture of one's organization (e.g., the sales organization is hard-driving), or the culture of a geographic region within a larger corporation (e.g., the Seattle branch office is more laid-back than the New York City branch office).

Although "group" is an important part of the definition of culture, being in a group does not automatically mean that the group characteristics apply to every individual in the group or that they apply to all group members equally. In addition, there are also subcultures within cultures. We often confuse culture and nation, speaking of those from China or Paraguay or Russia as a homogenous group, as if everyone who lives there has similar beliefs and values. Yet within nations there can be strong subculture differences based on variables such as religion, ethnicity, socioeconomic class, and geographic regions. Even researchers make this mistake and assume everyone within a nation is high or low on a particular value or belief (6). In research on human resource management, over two-thirds of the studies use nation as a proxy for culture.

Differences in values across countries *do* exist, *but* in the case of many of the values that supposedly differentiate cultures, much greater variability exists *within* countries than *between* countries. For example, while there are between-country differences (on average) in how kinship ties are valued, there is equal or greater variability within nations. In other words, people within a country vary as much as people across countries. Researchers have found that only 2–4 percent of the variability in a person's values is explained by their nationality (7, 8). This means that while countries *do* differ in terms of *average* standing on these values, most of the differences between people in values are not explained by their citizenship. Too often sweeping statements are made regarding how people from one country feel, think, or act, when in reality such statements are stereotypes and may not apply to many of the individuals from that country.

The findings are similar when thinking of the national origin of those residing in the same country. Some of the most commonly mentioned cultural values are individualism (i.e., emphasis on personal choice and interests of the individual) and collectivism (i.e., emphasis on the group rather than individual identity and interests). The common perceptions regarding standing on these dimensions in the USA are that those of Latin or Asian origin are more collectivistic than individuals of European origin. However, research actually shows that Americans of European origin are not more individualistic than Latinos nor are European Americans less collectivistic than Japanese Americans (8).

Considering the cultural homogeneity of a nation is important too. Some countries are monocultural, but many are multicultural (9). That is, for some countries, the country's average score on a measure of values is more representative of individuals in that country (e.g., Japan) than of individuals in those countries where the culture is more heterogeneous (e.g., the USA). In India, there are multiple cultures, such as the Gujaratis and Sindhis, each with different traditions, practices, and languages. Similarly, in China, there are different cultures such as the Hokkien and Cantonese communities, each with different cultures (10). Belgium is a bicultural state where some practices are national, but some are ethnically based. Sometimes practices in the French-speaking region of Belgium resemble those in France, and practices in the Flemish-speaking region resemble those in the Netherlands (11). Hence, describing individuals in a country as automatically possessing a certain set of values attributed to the country is indeed problematic.

Even in a monocultural society, there is a great deal of variation in individuals' core values (i.e., values that most members of a culture consider to be important) (12). Those who identify strongly with their culture tend to endorse the core values of that culture. Not all members of a nation have equal identification with the culture (12), and some individuals will not endorse core cultural values (e.g., they will be less collectivistic than most people in their country). Another way to frame this is in terms of *cultural fit* – how well an individual's values are aligned with those of the culture he/she is living and working in, regardless of whether he/she is a native (13). A person who is highly individualistic may fit a society where people on average are individualistic better than his/her own collectivistic culture of origin.

As we noted above, cultures can exist for groups other than nations, and the same false assumptions can arise. For example, companies, like nations, can have cultures too. Just as it is a mistake to think of the culture of a nation as representing all individuals, so too you must consider that within a large firm, there are potentially many subcultures (e.g., those in marketing may value innovation and change more than those in another function). Those people who are citizens of the home country of an MNC and work there may be more aligned with their country culture than the corporate culture while those people who are expatriates may be more influenced by the corporate culture than that of their home country or host country. Before a global staffing manager can determine the influence of culture on a selection process, he or she must identify the various cultures (country, corporate, or otherwise) that affect employees, determine the strength of the cultures, and evaluate the extent to which individuals are aligned with those cultures.

The box below summarizes our findings.

Good to Know

- Groups can be described in terms of shared values and beliefs.
- National averages in values do differ.
- There is a great deal of variability within countries in values.
- An individual's values may or may not match those of the dominant culture of his/her nation, ethnic group, or employer.
- Some nations and organizations have strong subgroup cultures.

- Some individuals will have a stronger cultural fit than others.
- Culture can be based on variables other than nationality such as ethnicity, geographic region, religion, or socioeconomic class.
- Cultural beliefs that are strong and widely held may or may not actually influence selection system acceptability.

What Are the Most Commonly Mentioned National Cultural Differences?

As we noted at the start of the chapter, there are many ways to talk about culture. A common way of examining culture is to look at values. Studies of cultural values abound, and whole books are devoted to explaining the differences. Rather than reviewing all these differences and the rationale for them, we have selected cultural differences that are well researched and have some implications for selection system design and administration. In the following pages, we will describe how these cultural differences should be considered as you plan your approach to global staffing.

Individualism. Individualism describes the extent to which a person has a desire for personal choice and personal achievement (14, 15). People who have high levels of individualism may enjoy touting their skills and experiences. A slight variant on this value is mastery, or the need for control over one's environment through pursuing individual goals (16). Individual decision-making is more accepted and individual goals take precedence over the goals of the group for those high in this value. While we wish to avoid the fallacy of attributing the same values to everyone in a given country, individualism is a more prototypical value for those in western countries such as the USA and less typical in eastern countries such as Japan (5).

How might differences in individualism be considered in selection system design and implementation? The implication for selection system design is to recognize the strong desire some applicants will have to talk about their past achievements and to build in the means for them to do so, either through the use of tools (interviews, biodata) that specifically request information on achievements or by allowing the demonstration of skills. Those high in individualism and achievement will favor selection processes that provide them with the opportunity to demonstrate their skills and showcase their individual achievements (15, 17).

Similarly, those who are low in individualism may focus on group accomplishments and have difficulty talking about their specific role. Employers who use structured interviews to evaluate KSAOs may find that interviewers have a difficult time teasing out what was done by the individual and what was carried out by others in the work group.

Because selection is inherently a process of differentiating among individuals, meeting the needs of people who value individualism will generally happen naturally in well-designed systems. In cases where all applicants are similarly accomplished (e.g., all possess a college degree; all hold a license or certificate), it may seem more efficient to skip a discussion of achievements in an area that doesn't differentiate; however, allowing some opportunity for applicants to note their achievements may enhance their acceptance of the system. Similarly, in selling a new system to internal stakeholders in individualistic cultures, it may be useful to highlight how the process incorporates individual achievement.

Collectivism. While people sometimes assume collectivism is the opposite of individualism, most researchers consider it a separate value. This value has two distinct aspects (17): *societal collectivism*, or the degree to which societal practices encourage and reward collective distributions of resources (i.e., a desire for harmony and equality (16)); and *group collectivism*, or the degree to which individuals express loyalty and cohesiveness in their organizations or families (16). East Asian and Latin countries are ones where there tends to be greater levels of collectivism (5).

In western selection contexts, jobs are typically distributed based on merit: those with higher levels of KSAOs are more likely to be chosen for jobs than those with lesser knowledge and skills. For a collectivist, treating all applicants as equally deserving may be acceptable (18). Hence, some resistance to selection systems that do not treat all applicants equally may arise from both internal and external stakeholders. For example, collectivist applicants may not like tools that employ adaptive testing (i.e., giving only certain items to an applicant based on responses to earlier items so that different applicants get different items depending on their ability), multiple hurdle processes that do not allow all applicants to be treated the same, or interviews that vary widely in length depending upon answers to initial questions.

Friendship-based ties can have different influences on staffing in different cultural contexts. In the Chinese cultural context, *guanxi*, or the social ties between people, and in particular friendship-based social ties, known as *shou-jen*, have traditionally played a role in HR decisions (19). In Australia, the concept of mateship, or a bond forged through overcoming shared adversity, has been found to be a possible influence on hiring decisions, even in cases of favoring a less-qualified candidate over others (19). However, recent research suggests that *guanxi* does not play as significant a role in hiring decisions as it may have in the past, in part due to the diminishing role of traditional Chinese values in society. Also, in organizations with formal hiring procedures that focus on job-related qualifications, *guanxi* does not appear to have as strong an influence as it may once have had.

In general, you should determine how your staffing systems might take into account social ties without overriding job requirements. For example, much research has shown that those with ties in the organization tend to be more likely to accept offers, have a more realistic sense of the job, and share values with those in the organization (20). Many organizations find that "friends and family" recruiting efforts result in more applicants who are qualified for the position. Incorporating employee referrals into a system allows for the consideration of social ties in contexts in which those are important, but this consideration does not affect assessment of qualifications (19). Research also shows that those who are high in group collectivism show greater preference for home country nationals than non-nationals and for males over females as these are often the "in-group" for organizational decision-makers (21).

Like individualism, cultural norms related to collectivism may make it difficult to measure certain personal characteristics.

Those who are high in societal collectivism may be reluctant to criticize others or take charge in group assessment exercises with other applicants in a desire to maintain harmony; group goals will take precedence over individual goals (22).

Case Scenario:
Considering Culture

In group assessment exercises for British Airways that evaluated cabin attendants' abilities to handle problems in flight, Japanese candidates tended not to take the lead or use the word "I." In the original scoring procedures, candidates who "took charge" were evaluated more highly, meaning that, on average, Japanese candidates were rated lower than candidates from other countries. Once British Airways realized what was happening, they modified the scoring procedures for the exercise and trained assessors to recognize other ways of expressing the competencies targeted for assessment (23).

Power distance. Individuals high in power distance defer to people at higher levels in the social hierarchy and are comfortable with status differentials and unequal resource distribution (14, 16, 17). Power distance is one of the most widely discussed and studied cultural values and is prototypical of Arab countries, Mexico, and the Southeast Asian region (5).

What are the implications for selection system design and implementation? Those low in power distance might expect a more participative approach to hiring (24). Members of a team might expect to participate in panel interviews or in final hiring decisions. For internal stakeholders, input into design of a selection system might be critical in cultures characterized by low power distance, and a lack of input could create strong resistance to adopting a new system. On the other side of the spectrum, some research suggests that the reputation of the organization and the status level of recruiters play a big role in applicant attraction in high power distance cultures (25). Further, one might mistakenly assume support for a global system in a high power distance culture where there would be a reluctance to ask questions or criticize those of higher status (26).

Like other variables, power distance can have implications for what is measured. For example, people who are high in power distance may have reactions to situational judgment items designed to measure service orientation that are different from those of people who are low in power distance. Because it may be more acceptable for a higher-level manager to solve a low-level customer's problem in one culture, scores on such a test may be higher in one country than in another. In another country, the cultural norms inhibiting interactions with someone of lower socioeconomic status or substantially limiting them may mask inherent tendencies toward service.

Uncertainty avoidance. Those high in uncertainty avoidance seek to reduce the unpredictability of the future (14, 17). High levels are common in Latin American countries, in contrast to the low levels observed in Northern European and Southeast Asian countries (5). In terms of selection system design and implementation, those high in uncertainty avoidance will be seeking information regarding matters such as what the process involves, how it will unfold and how long it will take. Designing systems that provide applicants from all countries with sufficient information upfront on what will occur in the selection process will help meet the needs of applicants who like to avoid uncertainty (27).

Applicants may also find some selection procedures more acceptable than others depending on their levels of tolerance for uncertainty. For those with high uncertainty avoidance, tests with clear right or wrong answers may be preferable to structured interview questions that could be answered in many ways. Further, applicants high in uncertainty avoidance are likely to prefer selection processes that provide more detailed feedback (28).

For internal stakeholders high in uncertainty avoidance, there may be a greater desire to look for concrete evidence of KSAOs in applicants than to look at "potential" (29). Selection systems that involve more components and require more extensive verifications of background may be preferred (4). Those high in uncertainty avoidance may be more likely to embrace the global standardization of practices (30). In contrast, internal stakeholders who are low in uncertainty avoidance may be less likely to endorse formal, standardized selection tools, more willing to test novel, unproven procedures, and tolerant of a great deal less information about an applicant prior to making an offer. In Chapter 2, we outlined the importance of basing a selection system on job requirements; such well-designed systems should be widely accepted by those both high and low in uncertainty avoidance.

Assertiveness and emotional expression. Cultures differ in the extent to which it is acceptable to be confrontational and assertive in social relationships (17). For example, assertive behaviors are seen as more acceptable in the USA. Countries also differ in norms regarding expressing feelings in public or maintaining composure and distance (8). These differences will play out in how interpersonal exchanges during the selection process, such as during an interview, are interpreted. For example, a weak handshake and lack of eye contact in an interview would be viewed negatively by an interviewer high in assertiveness, but in many Asian cultures, this behavior would be considered appropriate and respectful (23). Those raised in cultures with norms of low assertiveness may view discussions of explicit and ambitious expectations in an interview as impolite, although that is often viewed positively in western cultures (27). Similarly, emotional displays by candidates, even relatively minor ones, may be viewed differently by interviewers with different values (31). A Japanese manager who endorses neutrality in expression may see those from more affective cultural backgrounds as immature, whereas a Korean interviewer, coming from a more emotional culture, might interpret the more controlled affect of a Japanese candidate as insincere (23).

For the designer of the selection system, these differences in assertiveness and expression of emotions highlight the need for effective training for those interacting with applicants. Training for those who will be hiring globally should increase awareness of these differences and reduce their influences on evaluations. We discuss this further in Chapter 6.

Time orientation. Individuals differ in terms of the extent of their planning for the future and their willingness to delay gratification (25), as well as in their respect for traditions (10, 14). For example, people in China are often characterized as holding a long-term orientation (5). Thus many Chinese applicants can be expected to plan for the long term, to delay gratification for long periods of time, and to respect history and traditions. These differences in future orientation will affect the willingness to change selection systems on the part of internal stakeholders, the acceptance of lengthy selection processes in which the hiring decision is not immediate, and applicant perceptions of "novel" selection tools.

Consideration of future orientation in launching new systems will necessitate discussing traditions rather than ignoring them. Internal stakeholders' future orientation might affect the willingness to change the status quo and the likelihood of evaluating new systems in terms of their fit with customs and the extent to which they are designed to correct past mistakes (32). Providing orientation and test preparation materials to applicants to increase comfort levels with the selection process and explaining why tools are used will also be helpful in engendering positive applicant perceptions across cultures.

Monochronic cultures tend to view time as something tangible that should be saved and spent efficiently; punctuality is a virtue and schedules are kept (23). Polychronic societies view time in a more flexible and circular way and see maintaining schedules as less important than maintaining relationships (23). These differences in the perception of time may play out with internal stakeholders in terms of relative desires for efficient processes. Further, applicant reactions to timed tests, protracted hiring processes, or delays in hiring decisions may differ based on time orientation beliefs.

Analytic v. holistic thinking. Besides value differences, there are also cultural differences in cognitive styles. One such difference in thinking that has been well studied is the way people view components and the background in which they exist (33). Analytic thinkers see the world as made of separate components: they focus more on the individual parts of things than on the context. Holistic thinkers look at objects in context, notice the background more, and see the connections between things. This style difference is often considered to distinguish western (analytic) and eastern (holistic) cultures (33). In a selection situation, this distinction may influence how decision-makers consider selection information. Analytic thinkers may be more likely to focus on central information about an applicant and dismiss the rest as irrelevant, while holistic thinkers may seek to gather more information and be less likely to dismiss any one piece of information as irrelevant (33). Applicants who are holistic thinkers or who follow the norm in "high context" cultures may tend to provide too much information on resumes or applications in attempts to ensure that decision-makers have complete information about them (34).

As with assertiveness and emotionality differences, it is crucially important that those involved in the hiring process are trained in relation to different styles of thinking. However, it is important to remember that regardless of cultural differences, training regarding what information should and should not be considered is critical to system success.

Cultural tightness–looseness. Some researchers have considered how societal norms might differ. In tight societies, there are strong social norms for how to act, and norm violation is castigated; in loose societies, there are weaker norms, and norm violation is not frowned upon strongly (35). Japan and Germany are often described as tight societies relative to countries like Brazil and New Zealand, which are characterized as loose societies (35). Applicants in tight societies may appear more similar then in their background and experiences than those in loose societies, leading to some differences in the amount and type of applicant screening that might be required in those settings (35). In tight societies, selection systems may be seen as playing an important role in restricting entrance into an organization to only those who "fit" with the organization as a whole (35). Regardless of whether the behavior is the result of strong cultural norms or toler-

---

Tips:
Meeting the Needs of Applicants with Different Cultural Values

- Design tools and the scoring of tools with a consideration of common cultural values.
- Provide sufficient opportunities to note or demonstrate achievements.
- Explain very clearly any "differential treatment" of applicants (i.e., adaptive testing, multiple hurdles).
- Incorporate opportunities for referrals into recruitment.
- Provide detailed orientation and preparation materials.
- Train interviewers and administrators to recognize their own cultural values and the expressions of those values by those with whom they interact.
- Train interviewers and administrators as to what is relevant and irrelevant information to consider in decision-making.
- Explain to applicants why time limits are imposed on timed tests.
- Clarify the timing of the hiring process to applicants.

| **Tips:** |
| **Marketing Selection Processes Internally Across Cultures** |

- Note how cultural values were considered in process design.
- Clearly describe the need for and the fairness of any differential treatment of applicants (e.g., adaptive testing, multiple hurdles).
- Discuss how friendship and family ties can play a role through referrals.
- Provide ample opportunities for input into system design.
- Communicate throughout the development process.
- Emphasize the importance of training of interviewers and administrators in cultural sensitivity.
- Show respect for traditions in discussing needs and rationale for change.

ance for individual differences, the designer of a selection system should ensure that evaluations of those behaviors are job-relevant.

There are other cultural differences that have been researched that we do not discuss here, either because they have less relevance to selection contexts or because it is less well established that they differ clearly across countries. Overall, our message is that you can consider cultural values in selection system design without necessarily using different tools for different locations. In our discussion above, we have pointed out how many of the selection system features that might meet certain cultural values (e.g., providing more information on the process, having an efficient process, training interviewers) are good selection practices in general and should be followed with *all* applicants in *all* locations.

It is important to note that cultural differences do not generally change *what* is measured. If the requirements of the job are constant across cultures, then so too are the KSAOs to be measured. Instead, these cultural differences usually affect *how* something is measured or how the selection process is presented. It is also worth noting that there are multiple ways to accomplish some tasks and the preferred way may vary across cultures. In those situations, selection systems must take into account the different ways to perform a task.

What Do We Actually Know about Cultural Differences and Selection?

We have suggested that there are a lot of cultural dimensions that appear to have relevance for how selection is practiced in various locations around the world. However, we need to be clear that these are *potential* relationships – while they seem quite logical on the surface, very little data actually link cultural values and selection practices. One of us has been involved in two large-scale research studies regarding selection practices that do shed some light on these relationships.

The first study is one we have already mentioned, a survey of 959 organizations in 20 countries that was undertaken to see if national cultural values were related to the use of selection methods (4). In those nations with higher uncertainty avoidance scores, organizations tended to use more tests and conduct more interviews per candidate. While this study showed some variability in what were typical practices in different countries overall, cultural values did not explain a lot of the differences. It may be that economics or familiarity with certain instruments led to differences across countries in practices, not cultural acceptability (4). Indeed, the adoption of structured interviews over the past 10 years has been widespread as familiarity has grown globally.

In a second study, 1,199 individuals in 21 countries were asked about their cultural values and their perceptions of eight selection tools (36). Perceptions of biodata, personality inventories, and cognitive ability tests did relate to achievement values of individuals and in some cases to ascription values (i.e., beliefs that social status, titles, and the like should be valued). Overall, differences in perceptions of selection tools related to cultural values were not large, suggesting MNCs should be able to construct tools widely accepted across cultures (with some tweaking of tools in unique circumstances and detailed communications about the selection process). Further, country-level gross domestic product (GDP) was related to perceptions of fairness – those in countries without many employment opportunities tended to welcome testing, probably because it means a more equal playing field with regard to economic advancement.

There are a number of other studies that have explored the acceptability of different selection methods across countries (e.g., the Netherlands, Italy, Germany, France, Spain, Portugal, Singapore, the

USA, Greece; 30, 37, 38, 39, 40, 41, 42). Taken together, these studies show that applicants' reactions across countries are fairly similar and they question the use of culture to explain reactions. However, we should note that there has been more extensive examination of these issues in western countries than elsewhere.

In sum, these studies do suggest that there are some differences across countries with respect to what are typical or acceptable selection practices. However, you should keep in mind that cultural differences were not the only – or even the primary – reason for why these differences occur. The economic context appears to play a key role in whether applicants will react negatively to selection processes (17).

One area in which testing experts have established compelling evidence of cultural differences is in response styles on personality tests, interest inventories, and similar self-description measures. Specifically, individuals in some cultures are more likely to demonstrate acquiescence tendencies or respond positively to questions they are asked (43, 44). There are also differences in tendencies to use the middle of a response scale (e.g., choosing "neither agree nor disagree") versus tendencies to use scale extremes (i.e., pick a response such as "strongly agree" or "always"; 45). Finally, there is evidence that individuals in some cultures are more willing to put a positive spin on their self-descriptions (referred to as self-enhancing or impression managing; 46) whereas others are more likely to exhibit modesty in responding and may even underplay their qualifications. For example, Mexican applicants may be less self-enhancing and more acquiescent than US applicants (46). While these cultural tendencies do not mean one necessarily needs to use different selection tools in different locations, they have implications for how you interpret scores on measures and how (if at all) to make comparisons of applicants of different cultural backgrounds. We discuss this issue in more detail when we cover the topic of norms in Chapter 5.

Case Scenario:
Don't Assume Cultural Similarity

Latin America is often characterized as a set of countries that are culturally very similar. A recent research study of 915 individuals from four countries in Latin America (Venezuela, Mexico, Colombia and Argentina) demonstrated that this assumption can be faulty. They noted that although countries might have similarities in language, religion, and colonization history, there are differences that can affect what individuals value and how they act. These researchers found differences between these four countries in hierarchical values (e.g., power inequality beliefs, conservatism), suggesting you should be cautious before assuming cultural similarity in Latin America (47).

How to Judge Whether Cultural Adaptation is Needed

There is a wide array of dimensions on which cultures are assumed to differ, but we've also noted that while there are differences between countries in these aspects, there is also a great deal of variability within countries on values. You may now be wondering what should be your approach. That is, should you consider cultural differences as not great enough to warrant attention? Or, should you consider existing differences as relevant and design the system with differences in mind?

Given all of the research looking at cultural values differences, how should you approach selection system design? We suggest you:

- Do not make the assumption either that there are or are not cultural differences between the places where you do business. Investigate these with your local staff and with culture experts.
- Don't assume there are differences among your employees and applicants simply because there are national average differences in values. Your employees may be more strongly influenced by your organizational culture or they may have been attracted to working at your organization precisely because it embodies certain values that are different from those in the host country (e.g., those in a high power distance society who would prefer low power distance may go to work for an MNC that emphasizes participative management). Similarly, your applicants, by virtue of education or other opportunities,

may come to work for an MNC rather than a local organization in part because their values are outside the cultural norm.

- Recognize too the difference between a deeply held cultural value and the customary way of doing things. A person may not be concerned at all about avoiding uncertainty and predicting the future, but he or she may live in a place that customarily provides detailed information about all kinds of events and processes. Consequently, this person may expect such information – but may not necessarily value it.
- Consider how to build sensitivity to cultural differences into the process. Recognizing some of the broader value differences mentioned in this chapter, ask yourself how a process can be designed that provides opportunities for those values to be met for all applicants.
- Recognize the difference between variations in cultural values and variations in experiences. For example, citizens of a third world country may be just as individualistic as Americans on average, but they may have had such different life experiences that measurement of certain personal characteristics is affected.
- Investigate why a selection tool is not used or is resisted in a certain country. There are three common reasons:
  1. Unfamiliarity – It is just not the norm to use this approach.
  2. Infeasibility – Its use is not legally supported, the technology is not available, or the staffing context would make its use very difficult or impossible.
  3. Cultural unacceptability – Its use goes against common cultural values.

Our advice would be that if the reasons for not using a tool are #1 (unfamiliarity) or #3 (unacceptability), you should take the time to further investigate what modifications might enable use rather than dismissing the method outright.

One interesting point to note is that MNCs are actually agencies of acculturation and may lead to changing cultural values in a country. *Cultural hybridization* is described as a mixture of the local way of doing things and the new way when international practices are transferred to local environments. Cultures are reshaped through interactions with other cultures, and the combination of local values with those of the corporate headquarters. You need to be aware that over time hybridization may mean that selection processes can evolve to be less country-specific and more similar globally. A plan to foster such an evolution may be the appropriate way to move from country-distinct selection practices to a global staffing system.

We close with a scenario regarding cultural adaptation that is presented in the following box.

Case Scenario

Suppose considerable investments have been made in developing state-of-the art webpages for the recruitment of managerial talent. Expertise in webpage design, marketing, diversity, and recruitment was sought, and all features were extensively tested prior to roll-out. However, questions have been raised as to whether the pages are too headquarters-centric. In some cases, local HR units are requesting monies in this budget cycle for cultural adaptations for countries/regions. In other cases, units wish to use pages of their own design. Concerns regarding how local modifications work against development of a global recruitment brand are also being bandied about.

Having open discussions regarding what cultural differences are of concern and how those might be addressed while still projecting a global brand image is important to maintaining a universal system while respecting cultural differences. Some differences, such as differences in languages and the types of people portrayed on a website, can and should be made. Other differences should be investigated rather than adopted on the say-so of local units. As this chapter illustrates, there are a number of ways cultures tend to vary, and many of those can be accommodated within one system by making changes that would apply to all applicants.

How might knowledge of cultural differences have helped our Acme Global VP of Sales?

One problem the VP encountered was that some responses to a situational judgment test were not culturally appropriate (e.g., in some countries a female sales representative would not invite a new client to lunch to get to know him better). Having a tool development process or tool review process that specifically considers cultural appropriateness would have led to the redesign of such questions. In the next chapter, we will also talk about how piloting materials can help avoid such pitfalls.

Another concern the VP encountered was comparing the personality scores of individuals across countries. As we pointed out in this chapter, there is compelling evidence that responses to personality tests are affected by cultural tendencies. Knowing this upfront would have enabled the VP to do a more comprehensive review of the personality test and how it would be used before rolling it out globally. In the next two chapters we will consider just what elements might be included in such a review.

Think about this!

❖ When you refer to cultural differences, what do you mean?
❖ Have you been assuming that cultural values are held by everyone in a nation? Are you stereotyping by nationality?
❖ Have you assessed whether a difference in practices across locations is really due to culture rather than to simple tradition or convenience?
❖ How will you consider potential cultural differences in your development process? In implementation?
❖ What are the pros and cons of a slow evolution from country-specific to global systems through a process of cultural hybridization?

References to Chapter 3

1 Duignan & Yoshida, 2007.
2 Peppas & Yu, 2005.
3 Bhasin, 2007.
4 Ryan, McFarland, Baron, & Page, 1999.
5 House, Hanges, Javidan, Dorfman, & Gupta, 2004.
6 Tsui, Nifadkar, & Ou, 2007.
7 Gerhart & Fang, 2005.
8 Oyserman, Coon, & Kemmelmeier, 2002.
9 Bartram, 2007.
10 Bhaskaran & Sukumaran, 2007.
11 Brewster, 2006.
12 Wan, Chiu, Tam, Lee, Lau, & Peng, 2007.
13 Fischer, 2006.
14 Hofstede, 1980.
15 Smith, Dugan, & Trompenaars, 1996.

16 Schwartz & Boehnke, 2004.
17 Steiner & Gilliland, 2001.
18 House, Javidan, Hanges, & Dorfman, 2002.
19 Sue-Chan & Dasborough, 2006.
20 Breaugh & Starke, 2000.
21 Garcia, Posthuma, & Roehling, 2008.
22 Gelfand, Bhawuk, Nishii, & Bechtold, 2004.
23 Vance & Paik, 2006.
24 Groeschl, 2003.
25 Stone, Stone-Romero, & Lukaszewski, 2007.
26 Carl, Gupta, & Javidan, 2004.
27 Javidan & House, 2001.
28 Sully de Luque & Javidan, 2004.
29 Papalexandris & Panayotopoulou, 2004.
30 Bertolino & Steiner, 2007.
31 Nyfield & Baron, 2000.
32 Ashkanasy, Gupta, Mayfield, & Trevor-Roberts, 2004.
33 Nisbett, 2003.
34 Lim, Winter, & Chan, 2006.
35 Gelfand, Nishii, & Raver, 2006.
36 Ryan, Boyce, Ghumman, Jundt, Schmidt, & Gibby, in press.
37 Anderson & Witvliet, 2008.
38 Nikolaou & Judge, 2007.
39 Marcus, 2003.
40 Moscoso & Salgado, 2004.
41 Steiner & Gilliland, 1996.
42 Phillips & Gully, 2002.
43 Grimm & Church, 1999.
44 Smith, 2004.
45 Hui & Triandis, 1989.
46 Church, Katigbak, del Prado, Valdez-Medina, Miramontes, & Ortiz, 2006.
47 Varela, Esqueda, & Perez, 2008.

Suggestions for Further Reading

Ryan, A. M., McFarland, L., Baron H., & Page, R. C. (1999). An international look at selection practices: Nation and culture as explanations for variability in practice. *Personnel Psychology, 52*, 359–92.

Chapter 4

Legal, Economic, and Other Considerations

In addition to considering cultural differences when implementing a global staffing system, you would be remiss if you paid no more than lip service to the importance of environmental differences across countries, particularly economic situations, available talent pools, labor market regulation and unionization, and laws affecting hiring. These differences in context do not receive as much attention in discussions of challenges in global staffing as do cultural differences yet they are probably more significant (1).

In this chapter, we provide a brief discussion of each of these important environmental factors. Given that these change continuously and that discussing every country's unique situation is beyond the scope of this book, we provide you with questions to ask and information to gather rather than try to describe an ever-changing landscape. Further, because we are selection specialists, not lawyers or labor market economists, we focus on a high-level overview and suggest consulting experts as your situation requires more detailed information.

Local Labor Markets

Case Scenario:
Keeping Warm

Target's director of HR in the Asia-Pacific region, who oversees hiring for sourcing, IT and finance, notes that "Everyone talks about the huge populations [in Asia], but in reality there's only a tiny number of people qualified for the jobs you need [to fill] – and everybody's fighting for them" (p. 2). Target is a desirable employer in the USA, but with no stores in Asia-Pacific, the brand is not recognized by job candidates, so much more attention and resources must be devoted to recruiting to attract qualified candidates. Candidates in India often receive many offers and accept them all; hence, no-show rates on the first day of work are high (as much as 30 percent). Target uses a "keep-warm strategy" of keeping in touch with newly approved hires by sending information, making calls, and presenting small gifts for parents before the individual is due on board (2).

Most MNCs gather a great deal of information on the local economic situation before initiating business in various markets. They want to know if there is a qualified labor supply before they invest in the infrastructure critical to their business. When you are considering staffing in a particular location, you must determine how the labor market conditions that were favorable for business affect the design and implementation of the selection system. For example, if your organization built a new manufacturing facility in a location in part because of the availability of cheap labor, you need to identify the ramifications for the selection process in that location (e.g., many more applicants to process, potentially more unqualified applicants seeking jobs, less need to emphasize recruiting).

The local economic context will also affect applicant receptivity to various selection methods. For example, applicants may be less concerned about the type of selection method used in economically depressed areas, where individuals are more concerned about just getting a job, than in economically thriving locations, where individuals might not apply if a process is seen as either particularly difficult or simply different from the norm (3; also 4).

To make good staffing decisions, you should gather accurate information on what the labor supply for a given job is, not just the general economic situation of a country. Some countries that have a great deal of poverty also have a substantial, well-educated middle class. Some applicant pools are less affected by national economic downturns and have unemployment rates quite different than the national average. You also need to identify regional variations within a country and assess the potential effects on sourcing candidates and evaluating them.

Keeping abreast of changing labor markets is also important. The European Union recently proposed new rules to attract skilled workers to Europe. Currently 85% of the unskilled workers emigrating from developing countries go to Europe, but only 5% of emigrating skilled workers go there (5).

The International Labor Organization (ILO) has been interested in exploring the "economic footprint" of MNCs in the communities in which they do business (6). As part of your oversight responsibilities, you may need to monitor the effects of your business and your selection system on the local labor market and economy and at times adjust your staffing strategies, policies, and, potentially, your methods of hiring. For example, MNC expansion in Asia has led to escalating salaries (7), which in turn may affect recruiting strategies.

Best Practices and Common Pitfalls in Assessing Local Economies

Best Practices

- Consider how the local labor conditions will affect the number and quality of applicants.
- Identify regional and industry market trends within countries as well as across countries.
- Recognize that your organization's economic footprint may change the local labor market.

Common Pitfalls

- Ignore the economic factors that affect selection system design and assume the conditions are similar to the home country.
- Fail to monitor labor markets over time in different locations and hence fail to recognize change that has occurred.

Educational Systems

The KSAOs a job candidate has are often inferred from an educational degree, credential, or license (e.g., an MBA in finance, an electrician's license, a high school diploma). However, you need to step back from the educational system of the country in which the headquarters is located to uncover what educational credentials mean in other countries. Degrees or other credentials may not connote equivalent skill levels in all countries.

At a general level, a country's educational system influences the number of qualified candidates in the applicant pool. Countries with limited education facilities may have high rates of illiteracy. Educational systems that emphasize rote memorization instead of critical thinking can produce individuals with the same degree but different skill sets. For example, many organizations have struggled to find qualified applicants in emerging markets like China, Eastern Europe, and Southeast Asia (7) because their education systems are either limited in accessibility or emphasize different skill sets from those in the USA and Western Europe.

Further, the typical weight given in hiring decisions for various educational credentials may vary. For example, in France a candidate's graduation rank is substantially less important than in England, Germany, Italy, or Spain (8).

Awareness of the educational system will aid in specifying equivalent educational credential requirements across locations, developing appropriate recruitment strategies, as well as determining needs to hire PCNs or TCNs to fill positions in places where qualified applicants are lacking. In countries where the educational system does not assure levels of competence in specific areas for those with degrees, additional components should be added to the selection process to ensure competence.

Collective Bargaining

One source of frustration for some selection system designers attempting to develop global staffing systems is understanding when and how to obtain input and approval from various collective bargaining groups. A lack of understanding of bargaining and negotiating traditions can result in major bumps in the road. For example, Western Europe has greater collective bargaining coverage than the USA,

Canada, and Japan (1), so it is important to have an awareness of what role Works Councils (joint management and labor decision-making bodies) might play in the approval of the selection system. (Our Acme VP found this out!) Conversely, China currently bans the formation of independent labor unions (9), so there is little influence by this type of third party on the selection system. In addition, company unions in China typically share the views of company management rather than representing independent interests (10).

Awareness of the typical collective bargaining roles in setting selection standards and methods can guide the process of developing and implementing your selection system and help you avoid protracted negotiations and strong resistance to change.

Legal Environment

An effective selection system complies with the laws of the country(ies) in which hiring takes place. Concerns with legal issues related to selection fall into three domains: (i) discrimination against protected groups, (ii) regulations on hiring foreign workers, and (iii) privacy laws. We discuss each of these in turn.

Discrimination Regulation

To develop an effective selection system, you must know if local law prohibits discrimination against specific groups, who comprises the protected groups, and how discrimination is defined. You must also understand the implications of laws that affect your choice of selection tools or the way in which a selection system might be implemented. Although we noted in Chapter 1 that those resistant to change may bring up "legal necessity" as an objection to doing things differently, we want to emphasize how important it is that you proceed with a good understanding of the legal context for employee selection.

A recent review of the legal environment for selection in 22 countries provides some useful information (11), and we direct the reader to this work for specifics in each country. (See "Suggested Further Reading" at the end of the chapter.) There is some basis for legal protection against discrimination for certain groups in all of the countries examined in this review, but there are many different types of disadvantaged groups that are covered (e.g., immigrants, native peoples, racial minorities, women). Across all countries, the most commonly protected groups are those named in US law: groups defined by color, race, religion, gender, national origin, age, and disability status. However, many countries also protect groups based on political opinion, sexual orientation, and marital/family status, which are not a focus of US regulation at the national level. The table below notes groups afforded legal protection in the 22 countries examined in this study (11). Similar protections may be found in other countries not listed.

Good to Know:	
Disadvantaged Groups within Each Country	
Country	**Protected Groups**
Australia	Indigenous Australians
Belgium	Non-western immigrants: Moroccan and Turkish
Brazil	Afro Brazilians, women, disabled
Canada	Immigrants, visible minorities, First Nations peoples, Francophones
Chile	Recent immigrants from Argentina, Peru, Bolivia, Ecuador
France	Immigrant groups: European, North African, Other African, Asian
Germany	Migrant workers/immigrants: Turkish, Southern European countries, reimmigrants (Volga-Germans)
Greece	Immigrants: Albanian, Bulgarian, Georgian, Romanians
India	Within Hindu castes: scheduled castes, schedules tribes, other backward classes; Muslims

Country	Protected Groups
Israel	Palestinian Arabs, Druze, Sephardic Jews from Iraq, Iran, Morocco, Ethiopia
Italy	Albanian, Rumanian, Moroccan, Ukrainian, Chinese
Japan	North and South Korean, Chinese, Brazilians, Philippines
Kenya	Foreigners: Asians, Europeans, Muslims, less populous Kenyan tribes (Swahili, Kalenjin, Kamba, Kisii, Ameru, Embu, Maasai, Somali, Turkana, Taita, and Samburu)
Korea	Foreigners
Malaysia	Bumiputra
Mexico	Women, disabled, racial minorities
Netherlands	Non-western immigrants: Turkish, Moroccan, Surinamese, Antillean/Aruban
New Zealand	Pacific peoples; Maori
South Africa	Black (disadvantaged majority): African, Coloured, Indian
Spain	Immigrant groups: Moroccan, Ecuadorian, Rumanian, Colombian, Argentinean, Bolivian, Chinese, Peruvian
Switzerland	Immigrant groups: ex-Yugoslavia, Italians, Portuguese, Germans
Taiwan	Taiwanese aborigines
Turkey	Religious minorities: Alevi, Christian and Jewish Kurdish, Arabic, Armenian, Greek, Jewish

Continued

Country	Protected Groups
United Kingdom	Indian, Pakistani, Black Caribbean, Black African, Bangladeshi, Chinese
United States	Black/African-American, Hispanic/Hispanic-American, Native American and Alaskan Native

Source: Adapted with permission from (11).

With the exceptions of Taiwan and Turkey, evidence of intent to discriminate is not necessary to pursue a discrimination claim, so you must be prepared to monitor the impact of your selection system on various groups covered in each country's regulations (11). Disproportionate rejection of members of a protected class can create as many legal problems as a conscientious effort to exclude them. When hiring rates for groups are lower than what would be expected given their numbers in the applicant pool, most countries require some evidence of the job-relatedness of the selection system. As emphasized in Chapter 2, job-relatedness is a basic requirement for an effective selection tool and should not be a difficult hurdle for the well-designed and well-documented selection system. As our example in Chapter 1 illustrated, South African law is unique in requiring evidence in support of a test's validity regardless of the existence of differential hiring rates. The only specific selection method banned in any country is the polygraph, whose use is restricted in a number of countries (11).

The authors of this massive legal environment review also point out that there is considerable variation in the treatment of disadvantaged groups in selection systems. In the USA, hiring quotas (i.e., hiring a certain percentage of a group) are not permitted except when court-ordered, and preferential treatment (e.g., using different scoring procedures based on group membership) is not allowed. However, there is a great deal more acceptance of permitting or even requiring quotas and using different standards for different groups in the rest of the world (11). Hence, you need to be aware of what is legal in the places where your organization operates.

The table below lists the major laws related to discrimination (11). Major factors in determining the applicability of a law to a particular situation may include the home country of the MNC, the home country of the worker, and the local work site. For example, one country's laws might apply only to workers who are citizens of that country rather than to all the employees of a company headquartered in that country (e.g., US discrimination laws do not apply to those who are not US citizens *and* whose location of work is outside the USA even if they are employees of a firm headquartered in the USA; 11).

Good to Know:
International Laws and Practices

Country	Law	Employers Covered
Australia	The Crimes Act 1914 Racial Discrimination Act 1975 Sex Discrimination Act 1984 Human Rights and Equal Opportunity Commission Act 1986 Disability Discrimination Act 1992 Workplace Relations Act 1996 Equal Opportunity for Women in the Workplace Act 1999 Age Discrimination Act 2004	All employers. EOWW of 1999 refers to organizations of 100+.
Belgium	Belgian Constitution of 1994 Article 10, 11, 191 Law Equality of Men- Women of 1978 Antidiscrimination Law of 2003	All employers

Continued

Country	Law	Employers Covered
Canada	Canadian Human Rights Code of 1985 Section 15 of the Charter of Rights and Freedoms (1982) Federal Employment Equity Act (2004) Federal Contractors Program Pay equity legislation (federal and some provinces)	Federal government departments, crown corporations, and other federally regulated agencies and organizations
Chile	Constitution, Chapter 3 (Rights and Duties), Article 19 No. 16 (Freedom of Work and its protection) and Work Code, Article 2 (2002)	All employers
France	French Constitution of 1958 International Convention of the United Nations (1965) ratified in 1971 International Convention of the International Labor Organization (1958) ratified in 1981 "The law concerning the fight against racism" of 1972 "The law concerning worker's liberties in organizations" of 1982 Treaty of Amsterdam of 1997	All employers

Country	Law	Employers Covered
France (cont'd)	L. 122-45 from Labor Law 225-1 and 225-2 from the Penal Code	
Germany	Allgemeines Gleichbehand-lungsgesetz: General Equal Opportunity Law	All employers, except tendency organizations (e.g. religious organ-izations)
Greece	Greek Law 3304 of 2005, Equal Treatment Greek Law 3488 of 2006, on Equal Treatment between people in the Labour Market	All employers
India	Indian Constitution Article 15. Prohibition of discrimination on grounds of religion, race, caste, sex, or place of birth Article 16. Equality of opportunity in matters of public employment Article 39 Article 46 Article 335	Government entities, public sector organizations, and organizations receiving government funding.
Israel	Basic Law on Human Dignity and Liberty Basic Law on the Freedom of Occupation	All employers

Continued

Country	Law	Employers Covered
Israel (cont'd)	Women's Equal Rights Law of 1951 Equal Pay Law of 1996 Equal Employment Opportunity of 1988	
Italy	Italian Constitution of 1948 Article 3 Legislative decree 216 of 2003	All employers
Japan	Labour Standards Law of 1947 Law on Securing Equal Opportunity and Treatment between Men and Women in Employment of 1972 Law for Employment Promotion, etc. of the Disabled of 1960	All employers
Kenya	Kenyan Constitution Chapter 5, Section 82 HIV and AIDS Prevention and Control Act 14 The Persons with Disabilities Act 14 of 2003	
Korea	National Human Rights Commission Act of 2001 Equal Employment Act of 1987 The Act of Employment Promotion and Vocational Rehabilitation for the Disabled of 1990	Not specified All employers Employers of 500+ workers for affir- mative action clause Employers with 50+ workers

Country	Law	Employers Covered
Korea (cont'd)	The Aged Employment Promotion Act of 1991 The Basic Employment Policy Act	Government employees Employers with 300+ employers Not specified
Netherlands	Constitution, Article 1 of 2003 General Law Equal Treatment of 1994	All employers (besides religious, philosophical, or political organ- izations)
New Zealand	Human Rights Act of 1993	All employers
South Africa	Constitution of the Republic of South Africa of 1996 Labour Relations Act, Act 66, of 1995 Employment Equity Act, No. 55, of 1998	All employers except the National Defense Force, National Intelligence Agency, and South African Secret Service
Spain	Spanish Constitution, Article 14 of 1978 Law of Worker's Statute of 1980, 2005, Article 4.2 and 17 Organic Law for Effective Equality between Women and Men of 2007, Article 1, 3, 4, 5, 6 Law of Basic Statute of Public Employee of 2005, Article 14.i	All employers

Continued

Country	Law	Employers Covered
Switzerland	Bundesverfassung of 1999 (Swiss Federal Constitution) Bundesgesetz über die Beseitigung von Benachteiligungen von Menschen mit Behinderungen of 2002 (Federal Law for the Equal Treatment of People with Disabilities) Bundesgesetz über die Gleichstellung von Mann und Frau of 1995 (Federal Law for the Equal Treatment of Men and Women) Schweizerisches Zivilgesetzbuch of 1907 (Swiss Civil Code) Bundesgesetz betreffend die Ergänzung des Schweizerischen Zivilgesetzbuches – Obligationenrecht of 1912 (Swiss Code of Obligations)	Public employers All employers All employers
Taiwan	Article 5 of the Employment Services Act of 1992 Gender Equality in Employment Law of 2002 Equal Employment Opportunity for Aborigines Act of 2001	All employers All employers Public employers & private employers who are government contractors with domestic employees of 100+

Country	Law	Employers Covered
Turkey	Republic of Turkey Constitution of 1982 Article 10 Article 49 Article 50 Article 70 UN's Convention on the Elimination of All Sorts of Discrimination Against Women Article 11 Prime Minister's office circular of 2004	All employers All employers Public employers
United Kingdom	Race Relations Act of 1976 Sex Discrimination Act of 1975 Employment Equality (Age) Regulations 2006 Equal Pay Act of 1970 Disability Discrimination Act 1995 European Community Directives	All employers, trade unions, professional bodies, and employment agencies All employers, trade unions professional bodies, and employment agencies All ages, young and old
United States	Civil Rights Act of 1964, Title VII (amended 1972, 1991) Age Discrimination Act (1967)	All public employers and private employers with 15 or more employees Private employers with 20 or more employees,

Continued

Country	Law	Employers Covered
United States (cont'd)		state and local governments
	Americans with Disabilities Act (1990) and Rehabilitation Act (1973) Equal Pay Act (1963)	ADA covers private employers, state and local governments; RA covers federal government Virtually all employers

Source: Adapted with permission from (11).

Regulations on Hiring Foreign Workers

There is considerable variation between countries in terms of their rules and regulations regarding the hiring of foreign workers. Many countries' laws reflect the general goal of ensuring there are no adverse effects on the job opportunities for citizens. Typically, there are processes for obtaining approval for hiring and securing appropriate visas/ work permits and other work-related documents for non-citizens. You may be questioning whether this is an important issue to consider in selection system design or something for HR to take care of after a person is selected. However, the difficulty of obtaining work documents for non-citizens may be an important factor in deciding where and how workers are sourced, in making clear to both hiring managers and applicants potential hiring constraints on non-citizens, and in achieving efficiencies of the selection and hiring processes (e.g., time to hire). For example, in the USA, relatively recent changes in national security policies have limited the number of work visas available to foreign nationals and added substantial delays in obtaining them due to longer biographical questionnaires and added security checks (13). Microsoft decided to open a new software development center in Vancouver, Canada to place new hires who were denied H-1B visas by the USA (14); however, relocating facilities to address restrictions on immigration is not always a practical solution for corporations.

Tips:
Strategies for Managing Immigration Restrictions

- Time recruitment of new graduates to coincide well with granting of visas in a country.
- Rotate employees to other countries while waiting for visas to be granted.
- Match attractive candidates in your global pool with countries where they can get visas.

Source: (12).

Privacy Laws

Privacy laws in many countries prevent the transfer of personal information across borders, making it difficult to collect and use information on a global talent pool effectively (9). Our Acme VP was made aware of privacy laws regarding personal information when he tried to roll out a new system that relied on a single database. Although a review of country-by-country privacy law is beyond the scope of our discussion, the table below outlines some of the key principles in privacy laws across countries and their relevance to selection contexts. These principles are derived from the Organization for Economic Cooperation and Development (OECD) *Guidelines on the Protection of Privacy and Transborder Flows of Personal Data*. Similar principles underlie the European Union's Data Protection Directive.

As well as the three categories of laws and regulations mentioned above (discrimination, hiring foreign workers, and privacy), both multilateral agreements between governments and intergovernmental organization regulations also have implications for the workforce. In the pages that follow, we briefly discuss multilateral trade agreements, intergovernmental organizations, and nongovernmental organizations.

Good to Know:
Privacy Directives

Principle	Relevance to selection
Limits on data collection: Laws generally state that the purpose for collecting the data should be made clear, and data should be collected with the knowledge of the individual.	Organizations must inform applicants of how information will be used, limit use to selection purposes or specify otherwise at the time the data are collected, clarify what data will be collected.
Limits on use: Many laws note that any future uses of the data should be made clear at the time of data collection, or consent must be obtained for any other use.	Organizations interested in retaining applicant information for system monitoring, validation efforts, or employee development should clarify such use upfront.
Protection of data: Personal information should be protected from misuse.	Electronic systems for tracking applicant information must have safeguards to protect the security of stored information.

Multilateral trade agreements between governments (9) include agreements such as the North American Free Trade Agreement (NAFTA), the Association of South East Asian Nations (ASEAN) Free Trade Area, the Southern Common Market (MERCOSUR) for South American countries, and the European Union (EU). All of these agreements have workforce implications. For example, the EU has resulted in a major increase in labor migration across national borders of participating nations. The EU Charter of Fundamental Rights provides some common employment rights.

Good to Know:
Relevant European Directives

There are two European Community Directives that have a direct relevance for selection system developers and users: the Racial Equality Directive and the Employment Framework Directive. These are designed to give a common level of legal protection against discrimination in the EU. There are six legally prohibited forms of discrimination in the EU: discrimination on the basis of sex, ethnic origin, religion or beliefs, age, disability, and sexual orientation. A recent European Commission report on discrimination in the EU (15) suggests that many feel discrimination based on these personal characteristics is widespread, although there are also differences across countries (e.g., discrimination on the basis of sexual orientation is purportedly greater in Southern European countries such as Cyprus, Greece, and Portugal). Further, the report suggested that awareness of the existence of anti-discrimination laws was quite low throughout the EU.

Intergovernmental organizations (IGOs) can also have an effect on selection systems (7). The United Nations, with 191 member countries, is the largest IGO. It contains the International Labor Organization (ILO), which developed the Global Compact, ten universal principles for work, including labor rights. (See the example box below.) The Organization for Economic Co-operation and Development (OECD) has 30 member countries committed to a market economy and democracy. The OECD has "Guidelines for Multinational Enterprises," which provides a code of corporate responsibility. The OECD has also issued guidelines for privacy, noted above. The World Trade Organization (WTO) has 150 members and monitors employment trends among other responsibilities. Further, financial IGOs, such as the World Bank and International Monetary Fund (IMF), may affect selection processes through their influence on economic conditions.

Example:
International Regulations from the ILO

- International Labor Law – the Discrimination (Employment and Occupation) Convention, 1958 (No. 111) prohibits hiring decisions based on race, color, sex, religion, political opinion, nationality, social origin, or marital or family status. Managers should ensure that what appear to be neutral criteria do not inadvertently disadvantage certain groups.
- The Vocational Rehabilitation and Employment (Disabled Persons) Convention, 1983 (No. 159) encourages firms to develop a policy to eliminate discrimination against persons with disabilities unless legitimate reasons exist (person's inability to perform the job or firm's inability to bear the extra costs entailed in hiring a person with special needs).

Nongovernmental organizations (NGOs) are non-profit advocacy and human services groups (e.g., Amnesty International; 9). These are less likely to directly influence selection system design, but they certainly can play a role in advocating for workers' rights, influencing the local educational system, and affecting economic conditions as well as in shaping attitudes of local workers toward MNCs.

The challenge in navigating the legal environment in various locales understands which regulations apply to the MNC – many countries have laws that limit applicability only to foreign workers, private or public sector organizations, or government contractors. For example, in India, labor laws require that new jobs be advertised and a formal process of recruitment be followed in public sector organizations where external advertisements and recruitment agencies are used; however, many private sector organizations still have recruitment processes that are heavily influenced by social contacts, and recruitment is based on informal means such as word of mouth.

Further, a MNC based in one country that adopts local staffing practices in conflict with headquarters country law that applies to citizens who are temporarily working in that locale could face legal problems – such a situation requires careful investigation and legal counsel (12). A review of how US discrimination law applies internationally (12) offers the tips below, applicable to MNCs headquartered anywhere.

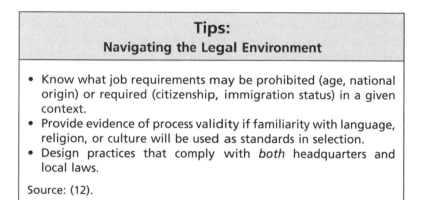

Example:
Laws Affecting Workforce Segments

In the United Arab Emirates, Yemen, and Kuwait, women are forbidden to work at night (16). Women need permission from their husband to register land in Zimbabwe or to start a business in the Democratic Republic of Congo (16). In most developing countries, women are three times as likely as men to be hired informally (receiving no benefits or protections; 16). Women are prohibited from working in dangerous occupations in Hong Kong, Vietnam, and Poland (17).

Tips:
Navigating the Legal Environment

- Know what job requirements may be prohibited (age, national origin) or required (citizenship, immigration status) in a given context.
- Provide evidence of process validity if familiarity with language, religion, or culture will be used as standards in selection.
- Design practices that comply with *both* headquarters and local laws.

Source: (12).

Keeping abreast of changes in regulations can be challenging. For example, in its summary of the ease of doing business in various locations, the World Bank (16) notes rapid changes and reforms in Eastern Europe and Central Asia. Although most of these changes relate to activities like the ease of registering properties, licensing, and credit, reforms specifically related to employing workers can have direct effects on selection system design and implementation. However, the most recent World Bank report (16) notes that the fewest positive reforms take place in the area of employing workers – while some countries have increased the flexibility of their labor regulations, others have made them more rigid.

Professional Standards

As the practice and science of employee testing grows around the world, more organizations are instituting testing standards and guidelines. For example, in the USA, psychologists who develop employee selection procedures are guided by the *Standards for Educational and Psychological Tests* (17) and the *Principles for the Use and Validation of Employee Selection Procedures* (18). Other countries have similar standards and principles. Representatives of many European nations participated in the development of the *International Test Commission Guidelines for Test Adaptation* (19). Currently, ISO 9000 standards for test administration are being developed. While none of these has the weight of law, most of them reflect the professionally accepted practice in particular localities. Consequently, you should be familiar with the professional standards for employee selection procedures in the countries in which you operate. Failing to do so might cast aspersions on your selection program and call into question its professional acceptability.

Example:
Standards Vary

In the USA, large hiring programs that evaluate many applicants often give only high-level feedback. A test taker may be told simply "You qualified" or "You are not qualified." When more than 100,000 applicants are tested every year, it is not feasible to give personal, detailed feedback. In contrast, in many European countries, professional standards emphasize the importance of providing face-to-face feedback and allowing the test taker an opportunity to see detailed results such as scores on each test in a battery or even the correct response to items. Such differences have major implications for system design and in particular for the relative costs associated with the system.

In summary, part of gathering hiring context information will be understanding topics in this chapter in each country – labor markets, educational systems, collective bargaining, laws and regulations, and professional standards. Your planning should include the time and resources for these efforts. MNCs can play an important role in changing conditions of poverty and discrimination in countries by adopting global codes of social responsibility and leading to increased convergence in laws and worker rights across countries (20).

Case Scenario:
New Country Checklist

In 1996, McDonald's was opening a new restaurant somewhere in the world every eight hours. McDonald's has worked to build cultural sensitivity into its HR practices while retaining a standard global approach to employment. When expanding into a new country, HR has a list of employment practice questions regarding local labor laws (e.g., restrictions on work hours or the age of employment) that must be answered. The company works with local attorneys to establish what policies will be and how they will be implemented. For example, McDonald's often works to introduce the notion of part-time work in countries where it is common practice to hire only full-time workers. Despite variations in hiring policies, McDonald's has common hiring practices. Selection systems are based on a profile of success for the job, whether entry-level or management, and involve looking at specific skills, general knowledge, and customer service skills. For store manager positions, people are invited to work at a restaurant for three–five days to try the position out before a final offer is made.

Source (21).

Our Acme Global VP of Sales would have done well to have read this chapter and done a little research before he launched into his global roll-out of a new selection system. If you recall, some of his problems arose because of concerns about different educational system norms, different recruiting markets, different collective bargaining arrangements, and different legal requirements. Identifying these differences first would have better prepared our VP for the objections that were raised immediately. Knowing these differences, he could have determined where he needed to develop alternative strategies and develop "work-arounds" and where things might be truly infeasible given local conditions.

Think about this!

❖ Are you fully aware of legal distinctions in different locations that could affect staffing?

❖ Are you attributing something to cultural differences that may in fact be due to economic or other factors?

❖ Have you considered how the local economic situation might affect selection system design and implementation?

❖ Are you aware of the comparability of educational credentials across countries?

❖ How is your presence as an employer changing future labor markets in each location in which you operate?

❖ Do you understand how collective bargaining may affect your hiring processes in each locale?

❖ Does your plan include time and resources for gathering information on economic conditions, educational systems, collective bargaining arrangements, and local laws?

❖ Are you aware of testing standards that are applicable in the countries into which you are expanding?

References to Chapter 4

1 Gerhart & Fang, 2005.
2 Cullen, 2007
3 Steiner & Gilliland, 2001.
4 Ryan, Boyce, Ghumman, Jundt, Schmidt, & Gibby, in press.
5 Colvin, 2007.
6 Schuler & Tarique, 2007.
7 McNerney, 1996.
8 Segalla, Sauquet, & Turati, 2001.
9 Vance & Paik, 2006.
10 The Wharton School, 2008.
11 Myors et al., 2008.
12 Posthuma, Roehling, & Campion, 2006.
13 Ivener, 2006.
14 Hansen, 2008.
15 European Commission, 2007.
16 World Bank, 2007.
17 American Educational Research Association, American Psychological Association, & National Council on Measurement in Education, 1999.
18 Society for Industrial and Organizational Psychology, 2003.

19 International Test Commission, 2001.
20 Chao & Nguyen, 2005.
21 Solomon, 1996.

Suggested Further Reading

Myors, B., Lievens, F., Schollaert, E., Van Hoye, G., Cronshaw, S. F., et al. (2008). International perspectives on the legal environment for selection. *Industrial and Organizational Psychology: Perspectives on Science and Practice*, *1*, 206–46.

Chapter 5

Best Practices in the Design of Global Selection Systems

Our Acme VP of Sales was well-intentioned, but he made some costly missteps. In this chapter and the next, we'll return to the points from Chapter 2 on what makes a good selection system and discuss how you can manage to achieve these while making your selection system a global one, using our VP's experiences as illustrations. In Chapter 2, we noted that a good selection system:

- Has a defined selection objective.
- Starts with gathering information about the context to support choices about the selection process.
- Involves careful development of each and every tool used.
- Takes into account how information from each selection tool will be combined and integrated.
- Has its effectiveness supported by data that demonstrate the selection procedures' relationship to the job requirements and work outcomes like job performance.
- Is not unfair or biased.
- Meets efficiency requirements.
- Fits the staffing environment.
- Can be marketed easily to stakeholders.
- Has processes for monitoring implementation in place.
- Is linked to effective recruitment practices.

In this chapter we will discuss how to accomplish the first six of these when using a global system. In Chapter 6, we will cover the remaining five.

Defining a Global Selection Objective

Although all of the basic questions regarding strategic objectives raised in Chapter 2 need to be addressed when going global, there are some additional issues you need to be sure to consider.

First, you must *understand the corporate imperative*. That is, what is the organization trying to do by developing a global staffing system for a particular job? Is the primary imperative to create efficiencies and reduce costs by eliminating redundancies in selection tools and processes? Is the ultimate goal to try to create the same global standards of quality in the people who are hired? If you are unsure about what the ultimate goal is, you may miss your target and make strategic choices that do not align with the corporate imperative. For example, if efficiencies are believed to be of critical importance, you may choose to use one set of tools globally; however, if these tools do not work well in all cultures, that choice may not result in an equivalent quality of hires across locations (e.g., due to lack of skills in the population in certain locales).

Second, you must *know the future strategic thrust* of the organization (1). A good understanding of the overall business plan and projected market expansions will help you understand what your global selection system must accomplish. Designing a selection system to be used in five countries with similar cultural values, economies, and levels of English proficiency is a different task from designing one to operate in those five countries with planned expansion within the next two years to two more countries whose emerging markets are culturally very different. Knowing the organization's future strategic thrust will enable you to design a system that can be more readily adapted when and if those anticipated changes become a reality. If you know your company is expanding into new markets, plan for their eventual inclusion from the start.

Third, you must *know the strength of the corporate culture* on a global basis. In an organization with a strong and unified global culture, communications of the aims and objectives of the system and its fit to the organization will be easier than in an organization that is comprised of many different corporate subcultures. If the corporate culture does not extend equally to all locations, the stakeholders in those locales may not embrace the same values and perspectives as those of headquarters. You may find it much more difficult to develop one system that meets everyone's needs, and the development and implementation of a new system will likely take more time and effort.

Fourth, you need to *establish a global team* (2). It is critical that various regions and countries feel they have input on the design of the selection system from the beginning. A global team can help find answers to many of the contextual questions and define the needs of each locale. A global team can also facilitate essential communications about designing and implementing a new system to all the stakeholders (3) and affect the ultimate acceptance of the selection system.

The team's composition will be critical to helping you gain access to the right people during the development process. Often, you will need input from current incumbents of the target job at each location, the managers of those jobs, and local HR representatives. Although the team need not consist of all these individuals in each location, members of the global team need to be able to effectively garner the support and cooperation of local stakeholders within their countries or regions. One of the key points made by those who have successfully developed global staffing systems is to involve many people in each step. Even if the numbers in a given location are small and unlikely to affect overall conclusions, their involvement will lead to the selection system design effort being viewed as truly inclusive and ultimately accepted (2).

Example:
Global Team Communication

One of us recently helped 3M develop, validate, and implement a test for sales representatives. The project began in the MNC's five fastest-growing markets, several of which were in the third world. The test was later implemented in a number of countries in the Asia-Pacific region and then in Western Europe. In addition to correspondence and project meetings necessary to collect job information, evaluate test questions, and set test standards, an email was sent to all stakeholders who had any interest in the outcome of the project every week for the entire duration of the project. The emails served to remind all participants what was needed of them and provide a status report for those whose participation was not immediately required. The emails were a critical factor in sustaining interest in the project over several years.

We should note that team members may vary widely in terms of their knowledge of and familiarity with the types of selection processes under consideration. If the current hiring practices vary tremendously across the organization, an initial step for the team may be some education on the characteristics of good testing programs outlined in Chapter 2. For team members to champion the new system in their locales and regions, they must first be persuaded to buy into the proposed changes so it is important to provide the background information and explain why change is needed.

One final recommendation regarding global teams for selection system design: both diversity of perspectives and also national affiliations are important to the success of the project. A team of psychologists designing the selection system may overlook the legal and economic conditions of the country. A team of HR professionals may lack the knowledge of best practices with regard to translation equivalence. The exclusion of line managers who will receive new employees may lead to neglect of the company's operational goals. Teams composed of members from the home country alone may not understand the particular legal and cultural barriers to some forms of selection. Diversity of team members helps ensure that all stakeholder issues are addressed.

We would be remiss if we did not note that there will be challenges in creating such a team and ensuring its effectiveness. (See box below for tips.) Because team members will bring their different national and cultural perspectives to the task of designing and implementing the new system, you should expect diverse views, disagreements, and the need for good procedures for resolution of differences (4). Building a global team may take much longer than a typical within-country effort.

How would defining an objective have helped our Acme VP? Knowing what the desired end goal for global selection is would have helped the VP develop the appropriate communication strategy to bring the other VPs on board. Understanding the future thrust of the organization would have prepared him for requests to expand the selection system to new markets. Being aware of where the corporate culture is not as firmly entrenched would have alerted him to which particular locations would likely evidence greater resistance and require a more hands-on approach to communicating. Most importantly, if the Global VP had started with a global team, many of

| **Tips:** |
| **Building an Effective Global Team** |

- Check and recheck assumptions of whether others have a good understanding of tasks and deadlines.
- Gain agreement on timelines that specify when input will be sought and encouraged and when the time for revisiting decisions is over.
- Show consideration in scheduling project events (e.g., create a global calendar of holidays and religious observances; distribute workload that involves after-hours communications; develop rotating call schedules).
- Clarify how and when individual contributions rather than team contributions will be recognized – and determine the allocation of credit between the team and the individuals.
- Establish agreement regarding the level of formality and affective expression in communication; encourage an understanding of differences in styles.
- Provide appropriate mechanisms for recognizing and respecting status while also allowing for recognition of individual achievement.
- Consider how to use technology to facilitate communications (e.g., satellite broadcasts, streaming video, Internet repositories, project software).

Source: (5).

the issues he faced would have been caught sooner and his plans for roll-out would have been more effective.

Gathering Information on a Global Basis

A very important early step in the design of a global selection system is to involve your global team in gathering the needed background information. The kind of information required has been discussed in previous chapters. In Chapter 2, we pointed out the need to gather information in three areas: the job, the hiring context, and the key stakeholders. Further, in Chapter 3, we stated the need to gather information on the cultural context. In Chapter 4, we discussed the importance of gathering information on the legal environment, the economy, collective bargaining constraints, the educational systems in each locale, and other factors like local testing practices. While the preceding chapters outlined *what* to gather, in this chapter, we want to highlight *how to compile* that information to best inform decision-making.

1. *The job*. The type of job information you gather will be the same in each location; however, you must use this information to decide if jobs are similar enough across locations to warrant the same selection system, or if differences are so great as to require multiple selection systems. We aren't going to supply you with detailed statistical analyses that can be used to make these judgments about the similarity of jobs across countries; instead, we want to convey how important these analyses are. If the jobs are different across countries, then a single global selection process is not likely to work. For example, if culture influences the extent to which job incumbents are engaged in making decisions about their work or if only supervisors make decisions (6), then a measure of decision-making skills will not be equally job-related and effective across countries. We advocate conducting job analyses of the job in each country – identifying which tasks are performed and gathering information on what KSAOs are needed to perform the tasks in each location – and then conducting a comparative analysis. Experienced testing professionals can help you design a thorough job analysis that will provide the data you need to make good decisions about your selection system.

In many organizations, jobs are similar across countries. A study of over 1,000 workers from 369 organizations in three broad job categories (first line supervisor, office clerk, computer programmer) in four locations found that, in general, the rank orderings of ratings of the importance and level of work activities and job requirements were quite similar (8). In another study one of us did, a comparison of the ratings of task importance and KSAO requirements for the same job across 10 countries found very similar ratings. Remember, however, that similarity should not be assumed, but demonstrated and documented.

Example:
Same or Different Jobs?

When the job analysis shows a difference in job tasks or KSAO requirements across locations, judgment is needed as to whether or not that difference is meaningful and necessitates different selection tools. Some examples:

- In some locations, the task of processing customer transactions requires the use of paper-and-pencil forms; in others, the task is computerized. A computerized simulation tool might still be useful in either location, as long as the computer skills required for taking the assessment are not great, and the skills measured by the assessment (e.g., attention to details; accuracy of recording names, product numbers) are relevant in all locations.
- In some cultures such as the USA, expectations about customer service are high; hence job requirements often include strong interpersonal skills and a friendly personality. In other cultures, "service with a smile" is neither expected nor required (7), and so these are not requirements for performing the job effectively. In this case, using a personality measure and/or evaluating interpersonal skills in the interview may be unwarranted in locations where individuals who could adequately perform the job as required in these locations would be screened out unnecessarily.

Case Scenario:
Using Job Analysis to Determine Similarity of Jobs

In making decisions regarding what assessments to use for sales manager jobs in their 400 hotels globally, Starwood Hotels went through an extensive process of reviewing job analysis information. The researchers compared the overlap in tasks and competencies for "sales manager" jobs in various regions (Asia-Pacific, North America, Latin American and Europe). Across these regions, tasks overlapped between 69 and 100 percent, and competencies overlapped between 91 and 95 percent. Starwood concluded that the same job title does not necessarily mean the same job, and that there was a need to focus system design on areas of overlap (9).

2. *The hiring context.* To determine the current hiring context in each location, you should explore the history of existing selection systems and the reasons for adopting the current system or for foregoing any formal selection system at all. Knowing that paper-and-pencil testing of a poor quality was used in the past in a location can give you insights into the receptivity of those in the location to testing, even if what you are proposing is of a much better quality. This knowledge may give you tips about who makes decisions about hiring processes in that location too. Knowing that a system may have been adopted when a site was expanding rapidly and knowing that the site is now hiring only at a very low replacement rate can explain why certain tests are in place even when they do not appear necessary. Knowing that an alternative to paper-and-pencil testing such as an assessment center was given serious consideration but was rejected because of concerns about successful implementation or cultural appropriateness can help you avoid a selection system that will not work well in the current hiring context.

We suggest the global team approach the process of selection system design by identifying best practices in each region so that they can be transported and leveraged globally. For example, Shell found that by considering how people are selected around the world and identifying the best practices in each location, the resulting global selection system was better than the best practice in any one location (2). Rather than adopting a selection system from one location and imposing it worldwide, as our Acme VP attempted to do, you should design a system that combines the best elements from wherever you find them.

3. *Stakeholders.* As we have emphasized, it is critical to gather information on what key stakeholders at each locale are thinking. In compiling the local view, you must be wary of looking at the "majority" view or the "average perception." You need to be aware of each and every negative view, even if they are held by only a fraction of stakeholders, to ensure success. Effective communication of your plans and your rationale for your approach may help overcome the resistance of that small percentage and ultimately may be critical to the success of the system in a particular locale.

4. *The cultural, economic, and legal context.* We've already noted that it is very important to do your homework on the context in which your selection system will operate. Understanding the legal or

collective bargaining requirements will make the parameters of a selection system clear, and details about the local labor markets and educational systems will provide useful information about the applicant population. And gathering information on real and perceived cultural differences will help in designing and implementing the process. We recommend you enlist appropriate experts to assist you in obtaining reliable information, particularly with respect to legal issues.

A key issue here is not to lose sight of this information as you proceed. For example, if a tool looks like it will be acceptable everywhere, but it will require some additional upfront explanatory materials to meet privacy laws in a certain locale, the project plan needs to build in the time, cost, and responsibility for the work involved with dealing with one locale's privacy requirements. The tendency is to simply say "We'll address that when we come to it." Needless to say, with global-scale projects such tendencies can create problems down the road when these many "little things" still need to be addressed as the date for the new system rollout approaches.

There is no doubt that our Acme Global VP of Sales would have had a much easier time if he had gathered information globally from the start. Establishing what elements of the job were the same and what diverged would have enabled him and his team to make judicious decisions about which elements of the selection system would transport easily and which would be less useful, before expending so much time and money on translations. If our VP had known the history of hiring programs in each country and identified the views of all stakeholders, he would have had some insight into the likely sources of resistance and may have identified non-US best practices that would be ripe for global adoption. A little effort to understand the legal environment in each country and the local economy, particularly with respect to the applicant pool, could have prevented some of the negative reactions about the testing program he implemented.

Developing or Adapting Tools for Universal Use

In Chapter 2, we outlined a number of considerations in choosing or developing a selection tool. In particular, we mentioned the psychometric properties of the tools, the cost and feasibility of administration and scoring processes, and the acceptability to various stakeholders. When moving to a global selection system, each of these factors requires an extra level of evaluation as there may be differences across countries that affect conclusions regarding tool appropriateness and effectiveness. Below we discuss (1) developing tools for global use and (2) adapting tools for global use.

Developing Tools for Global Use

There are some general guidelines for reviewing selection tools that can help with establishing their suitability for global use.

First, *avoid culturally offensive or confusing content*. This seems like a very straightforward suggestion until you realize there are many ways to perplex or offend someone in a given locale. Unless you involve members of your global team as well as cultural experts, it is easy to overlook a test item or an interview question that seems innocuous to you but may be odd or offensive to someone from a different cultural background. For example, a test that contains symbols like crosses and crescents may be anathema to some religious groups, and a picture of a pig might cause concern for Muslim job candidates (10). A less obvious, but still problematic example would be the use of life expectancy tables in a test of how to read charts in Italy, because talk of expecting death would be seen as unseemly in that country (10). In some third world countries where per capita income is especially low, affixing a price of $50 to a sweater might be seen as grossly unrealistic. A reference to the number of touchdowns in a football game in a math word problems test may baffle the applicant from a country in which football means soccer.

A second rule of thumb is to *avoid questions referring to specific measurements* that will require different formats across locations, unless knowledge of those measurements is essential to the job. If that knowledge is not essential, you should *ensure that you adapt them for each culture*. For example, job knowledge questions relating to money, distance, or time should be adapted for locations that use different currencies, the metric system instead of the English system of weights and distance, or a 12-hour clock instead of a 24-hour clock. A math word problem test that refers to yen may be difficult or even incomprehensible to an applicant who uses euros.

Remember, too, that a simple or literal translation may result in a question that is silly because it is so improbable. An item that asks how much interest is paid on a 6 percent loan on a house that costs $100,000 in the first year of a 30-year mortgage may appear ridiculous if yen are simply substituted for dollars. A better option may be to change the subject of the item so that the applicant must calculate the number of people attending an event if there is a 6 percent increase in attendance every year.

A third rule of thumb is to *avoid question types that do not translate well* unless that type of question is essential for assessing an individual's KSAOs (11). One example of this would be analogies questions, in which a correct answer would require not only an understanding of the meaning of the words but also of the context in which they are used and the relationships between them. These types of questions often do not translate literally across languages, especially those in which the words "is to" do not exist. Questions containing colloquialisms are typically problematic because they may not have the same meaning when literally translated. For example, a reading test that contains a passage about "checking out a book" from a library may confuse the reader in another language if "check out" is not translated properly.

A fourth rule of thumb is to *avoid country-specific topics* in reading passages (e.g., historical events, current events, national pastimes) to equalize the difficulty of the associated questions across cultures. A reading passage on the Battle of Gettysburg may be more a test of knowledge for Americans than a test of reading. Americans know what goes on at the Kennedy Center but may be unaware of what takes place at La Scala. A question that asks the test taker to calculate how many more quoits Herman has to toss on a hob to win the game if Herman already has 16 points makes little sense if you don't know what a quoit is, what a hob is, or how many points it takes to win a game. Consequently, the question becomes much more difficult and may actually measure an additional, non-job-related construct. In addition to arithmetic ability, the question may be testing knowledge about a somewhat obscure sport played in only a few locales.

A related problem is *differential appropriateness of behaviors* associated with what is being measured across groups. For example, things a leader might do in the USA differ from what might be considered good leadership in another country. One specific example of this occurs in an assessment center in which Eastern Indian managers would not refrain from interruption and not wait for a turn to speak, behaviors that might be rated negatively in a typical western assessment center (10). Another problem of this nature occurs in a situational judgment test question that presents a scenario in which a supervisor says something wrong in front of a subordinate. In some cultures, politely correcting the supervisor is an acceptable behavior. In other cultures (e.g., Latin American cultures), this would never be done.

Another rule of thumb is to *avoid any question that emphasizes the nuances in meaning of words or the difficulty of a word.* Many questions require comparisons of words to determine the relationship of the concepts. For example, a test item might ask if huge and large are similar in meaning, opposite in meaning, or are unrelated in meaning. In English, for most populations the huge/large question is not equal in difficulty to a question that uses the words gargantuan and colossal. Similarly, the use of uncommon words may cause problems in translation. An interview question might ask the candidate to describe a time when she had to ameliorate the effects of a bad decision. This question may be much more difficult than asking the candidate to "Tell me about a time when you had to fix a problem that was the result of a bad decision."

Experienced translators often struggle to find words of comparable meaning and familiarity, and in some cases there are simply no equivalent words in the second language. For example, in some languages (Hindi, Somali, Marathi, Setswana, Bengali, Urdu, and Uzbek), the concept of calf as a young animal does not exist. Hindi and Bengali do not have words for foal, and the Singhalese do not have a word for boulder. There is no word in Telugu and Tamil for blueberry. Even a common word such as "dress" cannot be translated in Marathi.

Adapting for Global Use

Often organizations are not interested in developing new tools for a location but in exporting a tool already used successfully in other locations. Doing so requires more than simply getting a translation. It requires translation *and* adaptation, and we want to emphasize the importance of this process of adaptation. *Tool adaptation* covers all activities related to preparing a tool constructed in one language and culture for use in another (12). There are several issues of particular importance in adaptation (12): ensuring translation quality, establishing equivalence across versions, and developing support materials.

Make the translations high quality
As we noted in Chapter 1, high-quality translations are costly and often time-consuming; however, it is a necessary step and a worthwhile investment. A poorly translated assessment tool does great harm: not only can the individual applicant be penalized in his/her performance because of a poor-quality translation, but the image of the employer can also be negatively affected by the candidate's (and local test administrator's or interviewer's) recognition that the organization is not knowledgeable about his/her language.

Careful attention must be paid to the selection and training of translators (12). They must know both the language *and* the culture of both the original country *and* the target country to ensure appropriate translation. In many countries, the translator must be familiar with differences in dialect within a country. Some subject matter expertise in the focus of the assessment (e.g., job knowledge area) is desired as the nuances of a topic can be lost on a translator unfamiliar with the subject. Finally, some training in test construction can be helpful so that the translator can help ensure the translated version is neither easier nor harder for the candidate than the original.

Example:
Translation Concerns within Language: Spanish Is Not Spanish

Differences within language across cultures are especially important when translating tests into Spanish.

- Guagua means bus in Puerto Rico but means baby or child in Chile, Colombia, and Peru.

Continued

- Verraco is a pig in Cuba, and a person who is tough in Colombia.
- Torta is a cake in Colombia, Cuba, Panama and Peru but a sandwich in Mexico.
- Perilla is a knob in many countries but a goatee in Spain.
- Saco is a jacket in Panama, a large bag in Spain, and a suit in Mexico.
- Banqueta is a sidewalk in Mexico and a bench in Spain.

Source: (13).

Once qualified translators have been identified, they need to be given specific instructions on the type of translation needed and the objective of the assessment itself. An explanation of the question types and the KSAO they are designed to measure is useful information for a translator to have. Other important instructions involve how to handle the issues they will invariably encounter during the translation process. These issues include:

- words or groups of words that cannot be translated because the word or words do not exist or make sense when translated literally
- instances in which the same word would be used to describe two or more of the response options to a question
- instances in which the translation of one word in the first language will require a large number of words in another language to convey the same meaning
- currency, distance, time, temperature and other measurement concepts that are not used in the locale
- questions that contain confusing or offensive information.

An important point for translators to keep in mind is that the question itself, once translated, should be similarly difficult and familiar in both languages. For example, the words "cat" and "feline" generally refer to the same animal; however, to most speakers of English "cat" is much more familiar than "feline." Consequently, the vocabulary used needs to be carefully considered.

Tips

To reduce translation costs and increase translation quality, follow these tips:

- Pre-edit. Condense and clarify as much as possible before engaging a translator. Cutting words saves money but it also makes it easier to translate.
- Banish jargon. Ask an outsider to review the documents first to point out words that are jargon, and then reduce or refine these, making the translation easier.
- Avoid metaphors and colloquialisms. Translations will not be as concise or accurate with them.
- Handle measurements (e.g., distance, volume, weight, time) and currency with care. Extra translation work may be necessary if the translator has to adapt a question so the measurements and currency expressed in the local metric still make sense.
- Avoid the overuse of verbal material. As translation problems are more prevalent in questions contain verbal material, attempt to limit the number of questions that are based on understanding the meaning of words and consider the use of questions that are not language-dependent (e.g., symbols, pictures).
- Screen for terms that are more familiar in some cultures than others:
    i. Sports terms. In the USA, there is an overreliance on sports analogies that can be difficult for translators or be perceived as odd or incomprehensible by those in other countries.
    ii. Historical and cultural events. Each culture has a unique past based on the history, language, and culture of the area. Sometimes references to them can be quite foreign to people of other countries.
    iii. Places. We are all more familiar with places and buildings that are close to home than those in foreign places. Foreign places are simply not as familiar, and references to them may make questions unintentionally difficult.
- Provide context for translators. Understanding that the material being translated is part of an application blank or screening test may help in choosing an appropriate term.

Sources: (14, 15).

Another requirement when translating tools is finding ways to proofread carefully. Your translator can frequently assist you, but someone must look at the final copy and make sure the translations are accurate. Proofreading a language, particularly one that uses an alphabet you do not know, is difficult and tedious – and sometimes just impossible. Languages that are read right to left or bottom to top pose special proofreading problems for those of us who read and write western languages. You need to make sure references like "in the box below" are correct and the box really is below.

Case Scenario:
Translation Challenges

One organization had a need to translate a test from Hebrew to five other languages (Arabic, Russian, French, Spanish, and English). Despite efforts to ensure the highest-quality translation processes, the team noted a number of problems that occurred in translation to Arabic such as these:

- While written Arabic is the same for all Arab countries, spoken Arabic is different from written and varies from country to country.
- Grammatical gender of words in Hebrew is often different from the grammatical gender in Arabic.
- Sentences in Hebrew usually begin with a noun while sentences in Arabic usually begin with a verb.

Source: (16).

The most typical method for adapting tools is to use *backward translation*, which involves the following steps:

1. The translator adapts the tool from the source language to the target language.
2. Different translators then take the adapted tool and translate it back to source language.
3. The original and back-translated versions of the tool are compared and reviewed.

However, even the back-translation process is not perfect – skilled bilingual translators can overcompensate in back-translating poor original translations (17). Our own experience suggests that you need multiple reviewers who are familiar with the content area and the job and are fluent in both languages. And, even then, reviewers are not going to be able to identify all of the flaws in the questions that make the routine field testing of questions prior to use a necessity (12). We recommend that monolinguals in the source language and monolinguals in the target language take the assessment after all the translations and reviews have been completed to identify any unclear material.

Case Scenario:
Translation Process

One of us recently developed a test for a European company and translated it into over 60 languages. Psychologists worked closely with translators to develop a process to ensure accurate translations. Rather than using back translations, we developed a process that involved the following steps:

- Create the first translation.
- Review of translation by a second translator.
- Review by a third translator.
- Review by a native speaker of the language employed by the client.

Translators were provided with detailed instructions. Specific instructions were provided to define how far they could deviate from the original English version and guide them in what words could be substituted and which could not. In addition, the instructions emphasized the importance of maintaining the original difficulty of each question. Examples were provided to highlight how various issues should be handled.

Often an organization will pilot test its translations in an attempt to ensure the translations are equivalent. Unfortunately, similarity or differences in scores do not guarantee similarity or differences in the materials. The differences may be due to differences in the translations, differences in the abilities of the samples representing the two countries, or differences in the populations of the two countries. For example, people in one country may be much more educated than the other, or the sample from one country may be more capable than the sample from the other country, even though both countries have equivalent levels of education. Such differences will mask the comparability of your assessment across locations. Indeed, the most challenging issue faced by selection system developers in emerging markets is not cultural differences among groups, but the wide variation in schooling and literacy across countries (18), which leads to marked differences in performance on the selection tool across countries. Similarly, you may find that fundamental differences in the environmental conditions affect group test scores.

To ensure the comparability of translations, you must conduct a complex research study that includes scores on your translated tests, measures of job performance and scores on marker tests that are known to be equivalent across cultures. Often, this is not done; instead, multiple translations of a single tool and checks of those translations are made to ensure all forms are "conceptually equivalent" in all language versions.

The International Test Commission (ITC) has produced Guidelines for Test Adaptation that can be helpful in determining if you have done a thorough job on adaptation. The box below highlights a few of the key guidelines that can serve as a useful checklist in requesting or reviewing work of vendors hired to carry out developments or translations of assessment tools.

There is a great deal of detailed information on how to use statistics to identify flaws in the adaptation process. Discussion of these techniques is well beyond the scope of this book. What is important is that we recognize that deciding whether an adaptation of a selection tool has been successful requires a fairly high degree of sophistication in statistics and is not to be left to a lone bilingual translator who says "the tests are the same." A testing expert can help you establish the statistical equivalency of your tests.

Good to Know:
ITC Guidelines

- Provide evidence that the language used in directions, scoring instructions, and questions is appropriate for all cultural and language populations for whom the assessment is intended.
- Provide evidence that the choice of techniques, question formats, and other procedures are familiar to all intended populations.
- Provide evidence that question content and stimulus materials are familiar to all intended populations.

- Provide evidence of equivalence of all language versions.
- Provide evidence of validity of the adapted version in the intended populations.
- Provide evidence of the equivalence of questions in all intended populations.
- Make aspects of staffing environment as similar as possible across locations.
- Provide administration instructions in source and target languages.

Source: (12).

Make sure you have evidence of the equivalence of the tool across countries

It is important to establish that what is measured by the tool is the same across versions. Although there are a number of statistical analyses you can do to assess whether this is true (see below), in the end you must make a judgment as to whether the evidence supports the equivalency of the different language versions of the tool. That is, can you use this version of the tool in different cultural contexts or must further adjustments be made?

As we noted in Chapter 3, one specific concern that is important in making cross-national comparisons of selection tools is the role of cultural differences in response styles on self-report measures. That is, certain groups are thought to have tendencies to use extreme options more while others are thought to use the middle of a scale, and certain groups are thought to acquiesce more and give more positive responses regardless of what is being asked (19). For example, if asked to what extent they agree with a series of statements, members of one group may "strongly agree" or "strongly disagree" with most

Definition:
What Is Measurement Equivalence?

Measurement equivalence refers to the extent to which two tools measure the same construct in the same way. When you are concerned about whether the same tool operates the same way with different groups (e.g., men and women, people from various cultural groups), there are some statistical analyses that can be done on scores and questions to assess measurement equivalence. The details of the analyses (such as differential item functioning, metric or scalar equivalence, use of multiple groups confirmatory factor analysis) are best left to psychometricians and organizational psychologists with these statistical skills.

You should make sure your experts can answer questions such as these with their analyses:

- Do the original and the translated tool measure the same thing in each culture?
- Do the original and the translated tool measure the same thing at the same level in each culture?
- Are response differences between groups a function of *true differences* between those groups or due to the fact that the measure does not work well with one group?

Be sure to ask vendors to provide evidence of equivalence (and remember this holds true of interviews and exercises, not just paper-and-pencil tests!). Ideally, such evidence would not be simply one single study; rather, it would be an accumulation of information based on examining equivalence in different groups, in different settings, and through different methods. Also, analyses of equivalence can be used to weed out questions that do not "travel well" even when the tool overall works well across locations.

statements, and another group may merely "agree" or "disagree." Awareness of these tendencies is useful. In some cases, these tendencies may lead you to use other types of selection tools that are less susceptible to cultural influences on response styles. In other situations, you may change how you compare the scores of people from one country to another. Response style differences can hide or exaggerate differences (19) between countries, so this needs to be considered when interpreting the results.

Case Scenario:
Response Bias Analysis

Personality instruments are widely used in South Africa, hence it is important to be able to assess when applicants are responding in socially desirable ways. This question of social desirability was examined in a sample of 34,754 applicants to various South African companies (20). The responses of 11 different language groups (Afrikaans, English, Xhosa, Zulu, Pedi, South Sotho, Tswana, Venda, Tsonga, Ndebele, and Swazi) were compared to assess measure equivalence. While similarity in how test questions worked within the various African language groups existed, several questions operated very differently in some of the African language groups and the English language group, requiring further refinement or removal of the question.

Source: (20).

Develop instructions and aids for administration with the same care devoted to tool development

It would be a costly mistake to put time, effort, and money into the translation and assessment of equivalence, and then to skimp on the translation of the administrative materials. Cultural differences and translation challenges are just as important in making sure that those who administer the tools do so correctly. We urge careful attention to this step in order to ensure that all tools are administered correctly and consistently and scored properly.

In addition to issues regarding translating and adapting selection tools, there are some other issues that you need to address regardless of whether this is a newly developed or adapted tool: cultural acceptability, familiarity, system flexibility, training for administrators and interviewers, and the combination of test and interview results.

Assess cultural acceptability

In Chapter 3, we suggested that culture may affect which tools are familiar to and preferred by applicants in different locales. Once again, we advise you to take a careful look at claims of cultural unacceptability. It is our belief that most high-quality selection instruments will be seen as acceptable tools for hiring in all locales because, by definition, high-quality tools are job relevant, and globally, people see job relevance as important (21). This does *not* mean you do not have to check word use in translations or make adjustments on occasion to instructions, questions, responses, and scoring as we have noted. But we do think – and a growing number of organizations have demonstrated – you can design selection systems that meet acceptability criteria everywhere.

Make sure that applicants are familiar with tool format
Sometimes those in a particular locale are less familiar with a given assessment approach and that unfamiliarity can cause anxiety and a lower level of performance that is unrelated to the skills you are trying to assess. For example, the ubiquity of multiple choice testing in the USA is not a worldwide phenomenon. Those unfamiliar with the format may be unclear regarding the appropriateness of guessing an answer or feel uncomfortable doing so. Asking an individual to participate in a "role play" may be unusual in certain locations. Another concept that is taken for granted in the USA but not in all other cultures is the notion of timed testing and the importance of speed. In many cultures, speeded evaluations are unknown, and test takers may be unclear as to the meaning of a time limit or unaware of techniques to effectively manage their time during the assessment.

You have several options to deal with unfamiliar question formats: you could balance the use of question formats or use only formats with which all groups are experienced. Regardless of the option chosen, we recommend that you provide high-quality instructions and practice questions for any assessment, so that any differences between applicants in familiarity (whether it be on the basis of country of origin or culture, or even within a country in terms of educational opportunities or other factors) will be removed. You should also carefully evaluate the need for time limits and the extent to which speediness in a skill is essential to job performance.

The use of online tool administration platforms has become very popular because they are an efficient way to administer a tool consistently across geographical boundaries. One word of caution is needed, however. Although the questions and the instructions can be translated into many languages, many of these platforms have buttons (e.g., START, STOP, BACK) that are not regularly translated and cannot be easily changed due to the software design. If you use a system in which some text must be in the language of the software developer and not the applicant, be sure to provide the applicant with aids that explain the text and time to practice. Moreover, we would advise you to plan for and negotiate appropriate adaptation of the platform by the software developers. While making such changes can be costly, it is important that your implementation not be hamstrung by this software design issue. Note also that many administration platforms that are written in English do not work well with languages that are read right to left or bottom to top. In these cases, you may be better off resorting to a paper-and-pencil tool rather than trying to adapt the administration platform.

In general, testing is more common in some regions of the world than others. A recent report on selection trends (22) found that the use of professionally developed tests or assessments was most extensive in Latin America (80 percent of staffing directors surveyed reported using some form of test), Europe (71 percent), Asia (69 percent) and considerably less extensively used in North America (37 percent). Although familiarity with testing is changing rapidly, researchers in developing countries have found that unsophisticated applicants struggle with concepts such as how to use a separate answer sheet or when to turn a page in a test booklet, let alone how to take a computerized test (18). Clearly, the way to address this is to provide preparatory and practice materials wherever unfamiliarity may be an issue.

Build in needed flexibility
Most organizations that have had success with global systems have allowed for some degree of flexibility in their selection program (2). For example, P&G found that policies that attempt to accommodate all variations due to legal, cultural, or other differences can become too complex, and it is better to allow for reasonable variation (2). Organizations may find that in order to tap the same KSAOs across locations you need to use different tools or variants on the same method rather than employ absolutely consistent assessment approaches (2). For example, IBM mandates use of a toolkit for hiring for a given job, but the company allows choice as to how the toolkit is used (e.g., who conducts the interview, whether prescreens are by phone or in person; 2). Another way of approaching this issue is to create common tools but allow for regional additions where justified

(e.g., add a test of English proficiency where needed, add legally required questions; 2). Note this is an upfront, agreed-upon, and justified addition, rather than a morphing due to resistance or a lack of understanding.

Give careful consideration to the selection and training of administrators and scorers
Sometimes the people who administer and score selection instruments will interact with candidates from cultures different from their own. A key issue, then, is to decide how they will be chosen and prepared for their roles. For example, should these interviewers and assessors have specific knowledge of the culture of candidates? How can they be trained to recognize and be sensitive to cultural issues (23)?

Example

Even a highly structured interview process can play out differently in different cultures. *Simpatia* is a way of behaving in Hispanic cultures based on a desire to promote smooth and pleasant interpersonal interactions. Hispanic applicants may show impression management behaviors such as a higher degree of ingratiation in interviews. On the other hand, the Israeli *dugri* speech pattern (24) is based on the notion that interpersonal relationships are healthier when you are very direct and truthful; manners can be seen as hypocrisy (25). An interviewer switching from Hispanic applicants to Israeli applicants or vice versa may find the contrast jarring and struggle to adjust his/her standards.

Individuals may differ in their *cultural intelligence* or awareness of cultural differences and motivation to act appropriately in cross-cultural situations (26). *Transculturals* are people who are high in cultural intelligence, have minimal cultural biases, and can make valid cross-cultural judgments. Whenever hiring will regularly be conducted crossing cultural boundaries, selecting interviewers and administrators who are transculturals will help you make more effective selection decisions that are not biased by cultural experiences. Selecting culturally intelligent administrators is not always feasible, but it is desirable whenever hiring will not be done locally by HCNs and cultural sensitivity is an issue. When you are not able to select culturally intelligent administrators, you should consider training them.

Definition:
Cultural Intelligence

While definitions of cultural intelligence vary, typical characteristics mentioned are:

- Open to alternative views and ways of doing things; flexible.
- Effective and comfortable when communicating with those of another culture.
- Able to suspend judgment.
- Skilled at recognizing behaviors that are influenced by culture.
- Knowledgeable about other cultures.
- Mindful and aware of environment.
- Able to move past stereotypes based on cultural values when interacting with those of another culture.
- Resistant to jumping to conclusions about others based on only one or two clues.

Source: (27, 28, 29, 30, 31).

Our Acme Global VP of Sales chose to go the route of adapting tools for global use rather than developing new tools. Clearly, the VP would have benefitted from investing in high-quality translations and establishing the equivalence of the tools across versions. As we have noted already, time spent on assessing cultural acceptability and familiarity in different locations would have led to preventing a few of the gaffes that occurred. Similarly, such upfront work might have led him to make some decisions about flexibility in locations where tool administration is particularly challenging. Some forward planning to consider the training of those who would administer and score the assessments would have been much more favorably received by HR around the globe.

Considering How Information Will Be
Combined and Integrated

In Chapter 2, we noted that organizations should make decisions regarding the sequencing of assessments, the use of compensatory versus multiple hurdle approaches, and other issues associated with integrating assessments based on both effectiveness and efficiency concerns. While ideally you would make the same decisions about ordering, combining, and integrating information at a global level, the realities are such that adaptations must often be made. For example, if sites for assessment centers are readily available and candidates are plentiful in one location, but in another the process of bringing candidates together is much more challenging, different decisions may be made about how early in the process the assessment center takes place.

Another important question you must address is this: *Will candidate comparisons be made on a local or a global basis*? When an interview is conducted, is the candidate compared only to other candidates from the same location or to some standard of an ideal candidate set centrally? If a test is used, are test scores compared to those in a global pool or only to those of other candidates in the region? Should local or global norms be used? (Norms are the scores of a representative and relevant comparison group of people that can be used to judge an individual applicant's score.) In general, if candidates come from a local applicant pool only, you must only use norms for that locale. If candidates come from all over the world and comparisons are made globally, then norm data must be collected from all international locations.

You can have multinational norms (across countries) that are global or regional; you can also have multilingual norms that are either multinational or within-nation when more than one language in the country is common (e.g., Canada, Belgium, the USA). Or, you could have multinational norms from two or more countries that share a single language (e.g., for all Spanish-speaking nations; 32) or from a clustering of countries identified as having strong similarities. The decision on the appropriate normative group requires careful judgment on your part (32), and the key to deciding what norms to use should be based on who is in the applicant pool. Local, national, and various multinational aggregations can be used to interpret assessment performance (33).

Some tools require special considerations when creating norms that are appropriate for your organization and your applicant pool(s). Although there are no hard rules on norm use, there is a substantial body of research that suggests that personality test scores differ on average across countries (34) because of cultural differences in response tendencies (as we noted in Chapter 3). Hence, developing appropriate comparisons for personality test scores (or interview ratings of personal characteristics like conscientiousness or openness) may require additional time and effort.

We should also emphasize again a point from Chapter 4 – the use of within-group norms on the basis of race is illegal in selection contexts within the USA (i.e., you cannot compare African American job candidates only to other African American candidates). However, in many other countries, such comparisons may not only be permitted, but they may be encouraged as a means of redressing prior discrimination and helping disadvantaged groups. Hence, the issues of candidate comparisons and the norms to use are ones that require investigation of the legal context.

Supporting Effectiveness on a Global Basis

Chapter 2 offered a review of the different ways to evaluate the effectiveness of a selection tool. When doing validation work on a global basis, you will follow similar procedures to evaluate your tools. However, in international criterion-related validation work, you must consider not just the cultural and language equivalence of the tool you are evaluating but also the cross-cultural equivalence of your criterion (or job performance) measure. That is, you may have a very well-developed tool and evidence of its measurement equivalence across translations. But your real aim in selection is to pinpoint who are likely to be the best performers, those least likely to turnover, etc. This means that you also need to consider whether "performance" means the same thing across locations and whether the relationship of the tool to job success is constant across locations. Performance is influenced by culture not only because individuals' values and beliefs differ but also because workplace norms differ from culture to culture (35, 36). The yardstick of performance may vary across locations:

what is successful performance in one location may not be acceptable in another. In addition, managers may vary in their willingness to make accurate performance ratings. Managers in some locations may be helpful in rating employee performance for the purposes of gathering validation evidence, yet in other locations, the notion of rating employee performance for such an aim may seem foreign or the motive of those collecting the information may be mistrusted.

The types of evidence of effectiveness you gather may not be the same in each location as some types of evidence may not be feasible to gather; however, significant statistical problems may result when different measures of performance or other work-related behaviors are used. We encourage you to obtain as much evidence about performance from as many locations as possible to help you make the best decisions about how well a tool is working and whether or not modifications are needed. Seek assistance from someone well-versed in statistics and performance management to help you equate per-

---

Case Scenario:
Assessing Effectiveness Globally

Starwood Hotels and Resorts operates in over 90 countries. In designing a new selection system for its sales talent, the company wanted a consistent set of global assessment tools. After development of a global assessment process, the implementation of the system was phased in over time to allow for opportunities for cultural adjustments, with English-speaking countries adopting the system first and then an additional eight language versions offered. Examinations of the quality of translations, the relative validities of different components of the battery in different countries, and the extent to which those taking the tests in a non-native language experienced disadvantages relative to those taking the tools in their native language were made. Although the different language versions of the assessments were found to be effective in terms of validity evidence, the assessment development team also examined which specific questions performed differently for different groups and targeted those for further refinement.

Source: (37).

Case Scenario:
Another Example of Assessing Effectiveness Globally

Procter & Gamble employs over 138,000 employees in over 80 countries. Since the 1920s, the company has been using biodata instruments in selecting employees. Recently, the organization sought to develop one biodata form for managerial jobs that is valid for all countries. A global team representing all regions was put together to generate biodata items to relate to the organization's global competency model. In addition to avoiding items on activities (e.g., sports, clubs) that might be country or region specific, the team focused on using general wording that would apply across countries (e.g., refer to top 5 or 10 percent of the class rather than to grade point average (GPA)). The team reviewed each item for cultural appropriateness. The global instrument's effectiveness was assessed in a validation study using seven language versions of the instrument (Chinese, English, French, German, Japanese, Spanish, and Vietnamese) and involving 6,000 job incumbents and their supervisors in 80 different countries. The validity of the instrument was improved by the use of culturally tailored algorithms for scoring; that is, a global scoring key was not as effective as regional scoring keys. Thus, while there is one form of the biodata instrument used, not all items are used for all cultures and not all items are scored the same for all cultures (38).

formance measures for a cross-cultural study and look for a testing expert to help you demonstrate the effectiveness of your tool.

Our Acme VP failed to provide evidence of tool effectiveness in multiple locations before he implemented his selection system; as a result, he suffered the consequences. Many of the users seemed to doubt the usefulness of the tools. A careful review of the system's effectiveness would have enabled the VP to handle skepticism about whether the system would be useful in various locations.

Fairness on a Global Basis

The fairness of a selection procedure is important for several reasons. First, a company wants to hire the best people possible – regardless of personal characteristics that are unrelated to the job. The capabilities of an organization's employees will play an important role in determining the level of success the business achieves. Second, the company wants to be perceived by the public as an organization that treats people fairly in all areas. Companies that are perceived to treat people unfairly in any area may not attract qualified people. Third, a company must comply with relevant laws. Ensuring that a tool is unbiased globally requires the equivalence and validation analyses described above to demonstrate that the test operates similarly in all countries and predicts your outcome of interest (e.g., performance, turnover) equally well for all groups. As our legal review pointed out, the specific subgroups within a country for which you need to evaluate fairness will vary, as will the legal requirements for establishing that you have an unbiased system. Nevertheless, ensuring your selection process is fair is important for business reasons too.

Think about it!

❖ Do you understand the corporate imperative?
❖ Do you have a good sense of the future strategic thrust of the organization?
❖ How strong is your corporate culture across locations?
❖ Who should be part of your global team?
❖ How can you best promote inclusion in the development process?
❖ Does your global team have sufficient grounding in basic concepts of selection system design or do you need some educational efforts?
❖ Have you assessed the comparability of jobs across locations?
❖ Do you know the hiring context history in each location?
❖ Have you gathered information on best practices throughout the organization?
❖ Have you gathered sufficient information on the job, the hiring context, the views of stakeholders, legal requirements, collective bargaining, educational systems, and cultural differences to inform your process?
❖ Have you reviewed tools you are considering for content that may be problematic on translation?
❖ Have you secured quality translation services, and done your best to prepare materials for ease of translation?

❖ Do you have evidence of assessment equivalence across translations and countries?
❖ Have you assessed familiarity with question formats across locations and provided appropriate instructions, practice, and/or training?
❖ How will you select and train assessors, interviewers, and administrators?
❖ Is there a process in place to monitor the consistency of assessment administration across locations?
❖ Do you have to make any adaptations to how information is combined and integrated at various locales?
❖ Will candidate comparisons be made on a global or local basis?
❖ Have you gathered evidence to support effectiveness on a global basis?
❖ Have you evaluated whether or not bias exists between relevant groups in each country?

References to Chapter 5

1 Harvey, Novicevic, & Speier, 2000.
2 Ryan, Wiechmann, & Hemingway, 2003.
3 Gilliland & Cherry, 2000.
4 Eggebeen, 2002.
5 Uday-Riley, 2006.
6 Shin, Morgeson, & Campion, 2007.
7 Donthu & Yoo, 1998.
8 Taylor, Li, Shi, & Borman, 2008.
9 Kaminski & Hemingway, 2008.
10 Nyfield & Baron, 2000.
11 Van de Vijver & Poortinga, 2005.
12 Hambleton, 2005.
13 Spielberger, Moscoso, & Brunner, 2005.
14 McKay, 2007.
15 Brislin, 1986.
16 Beller, Gafni, & Hanani, 2005.
17 Bontempo, 1993.
18 Frisby, 1999.
19 Diamantopoulos, Reynolds, & Simintiras, 2006.
20 Odendaal, de Bruin, & Roodt, 2007.
21 Steiner & Gilliland, 2001.

22 Howard, Erker, & Bruce, 2007.

23 Briscoe, 1997.

24 Katriel, 1986.

25 Blum-Kulka, Danet, & Gherson, 1985.

26 Earley & Ang, 2003.

27 Davis & Finney, 2006.

28 Thomas, 2006.

29 Triandis, 2006.

30 Ng & Earley, 2006.

31 Brislin, Worthley, & MacNab, 2006.

32 Bartram, 2007.

33 Hazucha, Ramesh, Bank, & Sevy, 2007.

34 Schmitt, Allik, McCrae, & Benet-Martinez, 2007.

35 Bhagat, Van Scotter, Steverson, & Moustafa, 2007.

36 Ployhart, Wiechmann, Schmitt, Sacco, & Rogg, 2003.

37 Tye & Snider-Lotz, 2007.

38 Pratt, Biga, Gibby, & Irwin, 2008.

Chapter 6

Best Practices in the Implementation of Global Selection Systems

Suppose Acme's VP of Sales has resolved all of the issues from our earlier scenario and followed the advice in this book. The new selection system is rolled out worldwide during the first quarter of the year. By year's end, it is clear that implementation has not gone completely smoothly.

- When the VP of Sales implemented the new battery, Country 14 was restructuring its entire sales division, and the selection program was not a high priority, and management in this country is not ready to implement in the first quarter. In fact, almost a year later, they have still not implemented the selection system.
- Sales managers in Country 15 dutifully implemented the selection system as directed; however, the managers don't really trust personality tests, and everyone knows that people lie on applications. Consequently, the managers in Country 15 put little credence in the results. Over time, one manager drops the entire selection system and goes back to her old way of hiring. Another drops the personality test but keeps the rest of the system.
- In several countries, the new selection system doesn't fit with other parts of the hiring process. For example, in several countries, recruitment is done by a third party, who conducts extensive interviews over the telephone. The candidates who are forwarded to Acme are then invited to the local offices for a tour and interview with the manager. There seems to be no time or place for the tests.

- One sales office is in Africa. Electrical power is sporadic so electricity for the office is generated from a nearby river. Because the premier university in this African country is in a different city, recruitment and testing usually occur there. However, even there, the frequent electrical outages often prevent delivery of the online parts of the selection system.
- A number of offices are in countries where qualified applicants are in short supply. One conscientious manager, who is required to interview three candidates, quickly found two candidates to interview, but it took him two more months to find the third. By that time, the first candidate he identified had taken a job with another company.
- A sales manager in Country 16 devised a test to evaluate a candidate's understanding of sales closing techniques. The VP of Sales was not interested in this test and told the manager to stop using it and start using the new tools. Angry, the manager adopted the new system, but continues to use the old one too.
- All of the data from the tests and interviews are stored in Acme's Worldwide Applicant Information Database, along with identifying information about the candidate. Because this is a global program, any sales manager can access any candidate's scores. Several managers have notified Acme that this database violates their countries' privacy laws.
- Country 17 hosts a start-up operation that currently has 23 people. The site is expected to grow rapidly, but there is no budget for selection processes. All the money is allocated to facilities and equipment. The sales manager in Country 17 can't use the selection system because he has no funds to buy the computers with video capacity.
- Scores from applicants in Country 18 on the personality test are unusually high relative to scores from applicants in other locations. It has come to light that the unproctored test has been posted on many student listservs and shared widely among potential applicants, with some schools and job placement agencies working with individuals as to how to best answer the questions.

You can see our VP of Sales still has a full plate of problems! This chapter focuses on best practices for effective implementation of global selection systems and ways some of the issues can be addressed.

You probably can come up with examples of well-developed programs, systems, and initiatives that were dismal failures because of either a partial or poor implementation. A global implementation requires even greater levels of planning than smaller-scale efforts to ensure success. In this chapter, we focus on some of the specific issues that have proven to be stumbling blocks on the road to global implementation of selection systems.

The transfer of practices in MNCs has received a fair amount of attention (e.g., 1). The success of transferring a selection process can be evaluated on three levels (2):

1. *Implementation*: Is the selection process actually used in the location? A selection process that is distributed around the globe but never used is not a successful one.
2. *Internalization*: Is the selection process viewed as valuable and trusted by the users at the location? A process that is adopted but not valued or believed to identify high-quality applicants is more likely to be abandoned (2).
3. *Integration*: Is the selection process a cohesive part of the existing staffing process (i.e., on boarding, training) in the location? A lack of integration with other elements of the entire staffing process can create more problems than are solved.

For all staffing systems, the goal is to develop tools that are implemented, internalized, and integrated with other HR practices at each site. The success of each process – implementation, internalization, and integration – is influenced by factors such as the governance mechanisms between headquarters and the locations, trust between key leaders in headquarters and the locations, satisfaction with existing practices, HR capabilities, and management of the change process (2). Thus, if you want a new selection tool to be not just implemented but also internalized and integrated at the local sites, you will have to do more than mandate the use of the new tool. You must convince the leaders in each location that the new selection practice works in their culture and can be easily used in the staffing environment in their location. You may also have to persuade the leaders in each location that the new selection system is better than the old one, particularly when the old system is well-functioning (2).

Occasionally, attempts to standardize selection systems globally can backfire and create more variation in practice. When a selection system is fully implemented in some cases, but only partially or not at all in others, a program that was meant to increase homogeneity ends up having the opposite effect and increases variability in practice (3). Integration and internalization are critical processes that ensure standard practices world-wide.

The goal of this chapter is to point out what you should attend to when planning your global implementation. In Chapter 2, we noted that a good selection system:

- Meets efficiency requirements.
- Fits the staffing environment.
- Uses staffing resources efficiently.
- Can be marketed easily to key stakeholders.
- Has systems for monitoring implementation in place.
- Is supported by effective recruitment practices.

In this chapter, we touch upon each of these topics and discuss how they relate to implementation, internalization, and integration of global staffing systems.

Being Efficient on a Global Basis

Case Scenario:
Enhancing Efficiency

Continental Airlines had an inefficient recruiting process in the USA, involving newspaper ads and open calls that resulted in hundreds of candidates coming to hotels in major cities. With expansion to international markets accelerating, Continental recognized this process would become increasingly inefficient. A new, totally paperless system was rolled out in the USA first and then around the globe within two months. Efficiencies have been achieved through extensive automated prescreening questions that remove unqualified candidates before the formal application. Hiring is centralized, and the automated global system allows a leaner staff to process candidates.

Source: (4).

An efficient system at a local level may not translate into an efficient system at a global level, unless careful planning and execution occurs. Myriad local issues may overburden and slow a hiring process, or poorly implemented centralized processes end up decreasing rather than increasing efficiency. However, we also noted in Chapter 1 that significant efficiency gains can be achieved when you use the same system globally in that development and implementation costs can be greatly reduced.

As discussed in Chapter 2, cost, time, technology needs, and the labor market are key factors in meeting efficiency requirements. Their importance increases exponentially when you implement a testing system at a global level.

For *cost*, you need to address:

- How much will it cost to build and maintain each of the variations to your selection system that are considered to be essential – culturally, legally, or otherwise? For example, if you want to use video-based situational judgment tests that depict native workers in each of your 15 locations, does that mean developing 15 different videos and budgeting for their maintenance?
- What costs will differ across locations? The cost of goods and services varies around the world. What is expensive in Western Europe may be cheap in Asia. An interviewer's or assessor's time may be affordable in Sydney but not in Brussels. A technology-based selection instrument may be affordable in Western Europe where the infrastructure already exists but unaffordable in Africa where it is still being created.
- What is your tolerance level for cost variability? That is, if test administration cost US$3.00 per candidate in the USA and US$10.00 per candidate in Germany, is that acceptable?
- Who will absorb the costs? Is headquarters able to foot the entire bill in those locales unwilling or unable to cover costs to make the implementation truly global?

For *time*, you should address:

- How long will the global development and implementation of a selection system take? The time to develop and implement a new system depends on the number of locations involved as well as the extent of the cultural and legal differences among the participating locations that must be considered.

- What is your tolerance for variability in the time to process candidates? Ideally, the time to administer the entire selection process should be as standardized as possible. Some components of the selection system (e.g., timed tests) must have no variability. However, complete uniformity in all components may not be feasible. In low-volume hiring sites, you may have longer lapses between application and assessment or between assessment and hire, so that HR resources can be used more efficiently. Competitive, high-volume sites may require quick processing to identify capable candidates and prevent them from being lured away by another employer. Providing a clear sense of where time gaps are acceptable and where time lines and limits (e.g., testing time) must be adhered to is important.

Technology facilitates consistency in practices, tools, and procedures (5) and encourages global efficiencies. The questions you should address include:

- How will variability in access to technology and the quality of the technology affect your system's efficiency? More than 40 percent of all Internet users are in North America, but the majority of the rest are in Japan and Western Europe. Eastern Europe, Latin America, the Middle East, and Africa combined account for under 11 percent of Internet users (6). You may find that the locations in which you will be processing candidates present no technological challenges, but it is important to take the time to assess the technology available – rather than assuming it as our Acme VP did. The technology that may be routinely available for doing business within an MNC may not be readily available for selection purposes or may not be accessible for applicant use.
- How important are the efficiencies of technology to stakeholders? Technology may be less important in certain cultures. For example, in cultures that value personal interactions like the Arab culture, face-to-face meetings or even telephone calls will be more valued than technological interactions like emails or messages on websites (6). In a slow-paced culture, instantaneous delivery of information

via electronic means is just not as important (6) – applicants will not be impressed with receiving information quickly.

- What adaptations or changes will be required to meet stakeholder technology requirements? You may need to change technology to obtain an efficient and comparable implementation globally. For example, IBM created a CD-ROM version of a web-based training tool for administrators so that all countries could obtain comparable training experiences for their staff even when easy internet access was not readily available (7).

For *labor market*, consider:

- What are the selection ratios in each location? Selection ratios vary for many reasons, including the differences in labor markets. Global system efficiency may be very different than local system efficiency because of differences in the applicant to hire ratios. In locales with low selection ratios (i.e., a small portion of people is selected from a pool of applicants), a system may be seen as cost effective and time efficient and be internalized and integrated more quickly than in locales with high selection ratios (i.e., a large portion of applicants is selected) whose leaders are frustrated because the system is not yielding as high a quality candidate. Our Global VP at Acme would have done well to recognize that different experiences with the selection system can lead to different attitudes toward it.

Overall, it is important to recognize that achieving global efficiency is a much more complex proposition than achieving local efficiency. Rather than forcing all locations to conform precisely, consider "tolerance bands" that define the acceptable limits of variation for each component of the staffing process. A system that leaves some locales outside the band of efficient operation needs to be closely scrutinized prior to adoption. Modifications for those particular contexts may be necessary.

One final important concern in discussing global efficiency is *what should be centralized*. Technology enables a great deal of centralization of hiring processes – you can have applications filled out on the Internet, prescreening tests administered over the Internet, and automated decisions made regarding whether or not candidates proceed to the next step in the process. Such actions can be handled from one central location rather than by each site. Later stages of the process may necessitate assessments be administered at different locations (e.g., interviews at hiring sites), but you can still centralize the collection of information on candidates (e.g., interview scores). Centralization is a good way of gaining efficiencies; however, decisions on centralization should not be made solely from an efficiency perspective. Centralization may be perceived by sites as giving up control and losing influence rather than leading to a better, more efficient process. Moreover, the cost of centralizing some processes may exceed the value of the efficiencies gained, and some processes (e.g., face-to-face interviews, assessment centers) may be more effective when locally managed. It is vital that your information-gathering process take into account this potential resistance to centralization and that strategies for best marketing centralization be considered in advance of rolling out a new system.

Fitting Staffing Environments and Resources around the Globe

Your global implementation efforts may be challenged by the variability in staffing environments and resources available for staffing across locations. Once again, planning for these potential challenges is vital. With regard to staffing resources, we've already mentioned the need to consider budgets and technology. You also need to consider the people who will be involved in administering and monitoring the system. You might consider the following questions:

- Do you have sufficient numbers of qualified individuals to administer and score tests and conduct interviews in each location? A good selection tool should not be included in a process if there are insufficient personnel to administer it to candidates. For example, requiring panel interviews or assessment centers will be problematic if there are not enough individuals on site to serve in the interview or assessor role as needed or a cost-effective way to get others to the site. A technical work sample requiring electronic repair will be difficult to score if there is no one at the site who can observe the work and judge whether it is done correctly.

- Have you developed a training strategy to address the needs of those administering the tools? For some tools that are highly automated, training might be a simple FAQ page (although even this is not so simple when you consider that you must review the document for cultural adaptation and do high-quality translations!). For other tools, training might be more complex and require considerable development time. It may take time to determine how individuals vary in their training needs and how you can most efficiently address that variability. For example, if a new system involves a structured interview process, the training required for those conducting interviews in locations where structured processes are the norm may be quite different from the training you need to give where structured processes are unfamiliar and perhaps even likely to be resisted.
- Does each location have the appropriate facilities for administering the staffing process? Knowing exactly where and how the process will be carried out is critical to identifying any potential obstacles to implementation in the staffing environment. For example, rather than simply stating that "testing must be conducted in a quiet environment without interruptions," administrators may need more specific guidance as they may see a corner of an office as "quiet enough" or may not view a ringing telephone as an interruption. Cultural differences in tolerance for noise, low light, heat or cold, and other environmental factors exist because individuals adapt to their typical surroundings. However, that does not mean that you should not strive for optimal conditions for candidate assessment.
- Have your policies regarding retesting, exemptions, confidentiality, test security, and cheating been developed and communicated? (Once again, plan for time, money, and effort for a cultural review and translation of these materials!) We noted earlier that cultural differences can influence whether applicants and administrators believe that exemptions should be made (e.g., for family members), or that retesting is okay, or that some kinds of cheating are acceptable. You need to ascertain what the views on these issues are locally and corporately and adapt your policy materials and training accordingly. In some locations, just communicating the policy is sufficient to ensure that it is largely followed; however, in our experience, there will be many places where policy will be ignored.

Hence, you need to devote considerable time and effort to educating your managers and administrators as to why the policies are needed and why they must be followed, particularly if they do not reflect the norms of the culture. You may also want to consider ways to monitor compliance to your policies.

Many an HR person has been surprised to find that a well-developed tool has "morphed" in operation. For example, interview questions that are not liked by hiring managers or ones that applicants have difficulty with are skipped or changed in certain locales. Time limits are created or dropped for assessments to fit the hiring context. It is vital that when a tool is adapted for use in other locations, extra, unsanctioned "adaptations" are not employed.

Clear, established policies can go a long way toward limiting these problems. A "help desk" or informative help webpages for administrators can also facilitate consistency in administration practices. Pilot testing of tools with local administrators can reveal what "shortcuts" and changes are likely to occur. Finally, building accountability for adhering to standards into the system is also important to guarding against problems.

Our Acme VP learned these lessons the hard way when he found out that the staffing environment in some locales created unanticipated challenges to implementation. In fact, this VP may be surprised when (and if) he actually audits what's going on in the field. The reports of his colleague may be the tip of the iceberg! Having reviewed the facilities, established policies in advance, and instituted procedures for monitoring would have curtailed at least some of these headaches.

Marketing to Stakeholders Globally

As noted at the beginning of the chapter, in order to be effective a selection system must be implemented, integrated, and internalized. Internalization of a selection system requires careful marketing to stakeholders. Accomplishing this globally starts with the information gathering mentioned in Chapters 2, 3, and 4 on the hiring context, stakeholder perspectives, cultural and legal limitations, and evidence of system effectiveness in different locations. You must convince your stakeholders that your selection system is an effective tool that identifies applicants who are capable of performing the job; that your selection system is an efficient tool that minimizes costs while maximizing the benefit in terms of better performance; and that your selection system addresses local cultural issues in a manner that is both effective and sensitive.

To sell your selection system, you may need to customize your message to the location. For example, you may need to emphasize improved applicant recruiting and attraction at one location and cost efficiencies at another. Questions of cultural acceptability may arise in all locations. Deciding how to communicate that the system meets internal stakeholder needs is covered in Chapter 2; once again, going global means additional communications tailored for different regions.

You also need to market the system to external stakeholders, particularly applicants. High-quality orientation materials will facilitate candidate transition through the process. Feedback can explain qualification status, strengths and weaknesses, and next steps in the hiring process. To complicate things further, applicants' needs and expectations may vary by location, and you may have to tailor the message and the mechanism for delivery by location. Remember once again that you must budget time, money, and people for efforts to develop these, investigate their cultural acceptability, and make good translations.

Candidate expectations of feedback can also vary globally. In some countries, rejected candidates are given little information on their performance in the selection process or reasons why they were not hired; in others, the norm is to provide the rationale for rejection, and, in some cases, to share scores on assessments and interviews, as our Acme VP found out. Individualized feedback can be challenging in a global selection system; it can also be a legal concern in some locations. To maximize consistency across global locations, feedback should be standardized; however, the feedback provided must also conform to local requirements and customs, making consistency difficult. Moreover, employers generally need to protect their investment in selection materials and want to maintain the security of them; you need to ensure that the feedback process does not compromise security.

Example:
Candidate Orientation Materials

Orientation materials vary from company to company, job to job, and culture to culture; however, there are some common elements in most. The following are examples of what is often included:

- the job(s) to which the selection system applies
- the elements of the selection system including
  - the order in which they occur
  - the KSAOs that they measure
  - the format and timing of each tool
  - the number of questions per tool
  - ways to prepare
- the timing of the steps in the selection process
- process for requesting reasonable accommodations for disability
- warnings regarding
  - cheating
  - protecting the security of the test materials
- instruction on
  - doing your best
  - guessing
- retest policies
- resource for questions
- information about the company and the job

Monitoring Global Implementation

Without mechanisms to ensure global consistency, small amounts of local tailoring can result in the use of a completely different selection approach from the one intended (8), as Acme's VP of Sales found out. Specifications and a mechanism for monitoring are needed.

Best Practices and Common Pitfalls in Monitoring Selection Systems

Best Practices

The specifics of what should be monitored depend in part on your particular selection system; however, the following list provides a good starting point of information to audit on a global basis:

- assessment scores (by country and, in many cases, scores by legally protected groups within a country)
- adherence to assessment instructions and time limits
- procedures for recording scores
- administration policies and procedures, including test exemptions and waivers
- training for administrators, scorers, test data base managers, and interviewers
- anomalies in assessment sessions (e.g., problems in environment like noise and temperature, administrator deviations from expected assessment conditions)
- security practices
- procedures to protect the confidentiality of scores
- candidate reactions to selection tools
- feedback procedures
- distribution of orientation materials
- candidate sourcing
- time-to-hire (from application to hiring and/or from ad placement to position filled)
- yield or selection ratios
- yield by source

Common Pitfalls

- No records are kept, so that thorough auditing is impossible.
- No systematic tracking is done but assumptions are made based on perceptions of how well the system is working.
- Information to be monitored is not systematically recorded so differences appear across locations due to a lack of care in information gathering rather than to true differences in effectiveness.
- Definitions of what is to be monitored are not agreed upon or communicated; thus, the information gathered is not the same at each location.

Regular audits of selection practices may also be helpful in large-scale and far-flung operations. Data tracking may hint at when and where "drift" is occurring; actually observing how the process is being administered at various sites can provide a great deal of insight – not only into process morphing, but also into areas in which the system can be improved or cultural accommodation may be needed.

Having pointed out the need to monitor for deviations from planned practice, we would be remiss if we didn't mention how one should deal with uncovered deviations. We urge you to take some time to investigate why the deviation from policy or system practice is occurring – is there something you missed in all of your information gathering that indicates that this is indeed a legitimate need for a variation in the system? If not, investigate whether factors might have prevented a full implementation of the system (e.g., sources of resistance not attended to earlier) and address those. Simply ordering a correction of a deviation does not address why it is happening in the first place and will likely lead to less rather than more support for the system.

We also want to emphasize the need to *monitor test security*. As noted earlier, there are cultural differences in beliefs regarding the appropriateness of sharing answers to screening tests and interview questions. Having invested much time and money into a selection system, you should also put time and money into ensuring that the investment is safeguarded so that it will continue to be effective.

Tips:
Preventing Security Breaches
• Limit access to tools. • Verify candidate identities. • Monitor test administration sessions. • Establish clear retesting policies. • Conduct security audits.

Global Recruiting

A selection system's efficiency is dependent on the applicant pool to be processed. Recruiting is integral to selection system success, and so attention should be paid to the same issues in recruitment materials and practices that have been noted as important for selection tools.

Methods of attracting candidates may need to differ from country to country. National newspapers are used for recruiting middle-level managers in some countries but not in others where national newspapers are not prevalent (e.g., the USA; 9). North Americans made more use of online job boards in recruiting; in Asia, newsprint ads were used more often; and in Australia, recruiters were more likely to use search firms than in other regions (10). Hiring from competitors is common in Taiwan but is more taboo in Japan (11).

In a global market, the familiarity, reputation, and image of your organization may vary enormously from region to region; hence, *recruitment activities may need to vary* to create the type and level of employer knowledge desired (i.e., a familiar organization with a positive reputation in one locale may engage in more and different recruitment activities in another locale where the firm is less well known or not as positively regarded; 12). One interesting idea is the cross-border referral program at Deloitte, which rewards employees for successful referrals of overseas colleagues (13).

Many argue that individuals prefer websites targeting their country and suggest *websites be culturally adapted* to enhance attraction (14). Organizations must work to project a global brand image while also making appropriate cultural adaptations (12). For example, Deloitte has one central website for employment and specific sites with information on offices in over 90 countries that is locally managed to avoid the situation in which "a person in China comes to the site and sees a photograph of someone who doesn't look like they're from China" (13, p. 34).

Further, organizations are often concerned about the *portrayal of a diverse workforce* in recruitment ads (e.g., 15, 16). On a global basis, this would extend beyond considerations of racial/ethnic and gender diversity to diversity of culture (e.g., through dress and other observable indicators of culture; 12).

Timing of recruitment may vary. In Japan, there is a yearly recruitment process for new school graduates in April rather than recruitment throughout the year (5, 11). In other countries like the USA, colleges and universities produce graduates throughout the year. In some countries, "gap years" are either required or a very popular choice. For example, Israel currently requires people to carry out two years in the military services. In countries such as Britain, Australia, and the Netherlands, many young people take a year to work or travel between secondary school and college.

Finally, multinational organizations are often concerned with recruiting individuals who are *willing to relocate* (17) and have the *capacity to work in other cultures*. We return to our point in Chapter 2 about providing applicants with the necessary information to understand job requirements and to assess their own fit. If cultural adaptability is a job requirement, then developing tools for assessing that ability should be part of the selection process. In addition to a targeted recruitment effort, some means of identifying those who can work well in other cultures is needed. Also, we noted in Chapter 1 that organizations may differ in desired reliance on PCNs, HCNs, and TCNs; working to achieve an acceptable balance may entail considerable effort.

Example:
Selecting People for Work in Other Cultures

Many companies try to evaluate their employees' ability to adapt to other cultures and perform well despite the differences in work environment. Some companies assess "cultural intelligence adaptability" (as defined in Chapter 5) and evaluate only the employee, assessing whether the person is flexible, adaptable, and tolerant. Other companies evaluate the entire family unit and look for factors that make cultural adaptation difficult, such as school-aged children who are reluctant to leave their social circles and employed spouses who want to find work. Often companies use realistic job previews to provide the potential expatriate and his or her family with information not only about the job but also about the culture in which the family will live and work.

Outsourcing

After reading Chapters 5 and 6, you may feel overwhelmed with all the things you need to do. In closing, we want to raise one alternative to managing the development and implementation of a global staffing and selection system that is sometimes used: outsourcing. Because global staffing systems require an array of experts in different areas, using a firm that specializes in this work can be an effective choice. Although large MNCs may have many employees, they may not have recruitment specialists in every country, with experience of developing and validating tools, translating tests and materials, implementing change, and so on.

Despite the appeal of giving the problem to someone else, caution is advised. Like your company, few staffing companies have expertise in all the areas required in all the places needed. They may not understand your jobs and business, or have personnel on the ground where you need them. Even firms that specialize in just one area may not be knowledgeable about all the geographic areas in which you plan to do business. And firms that specialize in a geographic area may not be able to perform all the functions you need.

If outsourcing is the route you choose to follow, do your due diligence on the company's capabilities and make sure your contract protects your interests.

Tips:
Considerations in Outsourcing System Development and Implementation

- Find out where the company has done business before.
- Investigate what the firm's capabilities are.
- Ask if they use subcontractors and how they manage subcontractor performance.
- Be sure your contract has specific service levels and a plan for measuring how they are met.
- Set dates for the completion of tasks.
- Ask to meet the personnel who will work on your account.
- Ask for the right to approve the personnel who work on your contract.
- Set up a monitoring process and check points.

Before ending this chapter, we would like to devote a little attention to defining what must be common across locations and what can vary for you to still be able to claim a system as global. As we noted earlier, you likely will need to allow some variation in practices to bend to local cultures, to meet legal requirements, and to fit staffing environments. On occasion, components (e.g., specific tests) may be added to or removed from locations where they are deemed infeasible or inappropriate. We would argue that a system can be global if its aims, objectives, and general structures are common worldwide, even if the elements of the system do indeed look different in different places. Our point is that the system is developed from a global perspective and with a global goal and that variation is carefully considered and purposefully allowed rather than haphazardly occurring.

Think about it!

❖ Are you focused solely on implementation, or are you making efforts to ensure internalization and integration?

❖ Have you established "tolerance bands" for system efficiency across locations?

❖ Have you evaluated cost, time, technology and labor market differences across locations and factored those into decision-making, planning and budgeting?

❖ Have you decided what should be centralized and what should be locally administered and maintained? Have you considered how best to market any centralization efforts?

❖ Do you have sufficient numbers of individuals to administer tests and/or conduct interviews in each location?

❖ Have you developed a training strategy to address needs?

❖ Have locations been reviewed for the appropriateness of the environment for administering the staffing process?

❖ Have your policies regarding retesting, exemptions, confidentiality, test security and cheating been developed and communicated?

❖ Have you evaluated candidate expectations regarding feedback and determined what your feedback practices will be?

❖ Have you established clear criteria regarding what you wish to monitor after implementation, who will do the monitoring, and how the data will be maintained?

❖ Are you planning a regular process of auditing system implementation?

❖ What mechanisms do you have in place to ensure tool security?

❖ Have you considered any need for variation in recruiting materials and activities to account for cultural and national differences?

References to Chapter 6

1 Kostova & Roth, 2002.
2 Bjorkman & Lervik, 2007.
3 Edwards, Colling, & Ferner, 2007.
4 Hansen, 2006.
5 Farndale & Paauwe, 2007.
6 Yasin & Yavas, 2007.
7 Wiechmann, Ryan, & Hemingway, 2003.
8 Eggebeen, 2002.
9 Nyfield & Baron, 2000.
10 Howard, Erker, & Bruce, 2007.
11 Huo, Huang, & Napier, 2002.
12 Ryan & Delany, in press.
13 Brandel 2006.
14 Baack & Singh, 2007.
15 Avery, Hernandez, & Hebl, 2004.
16 Perkins, Thomas, & Taylor, 2000.
17 Borstorff, Harris, Field, & Giles, 1997.

Chapter 7

Final Thoughts

In this book, we described a beleaguered Global VP, whose good intentions regarding a worldwide selection system led to lots of negative reactions and headaches. The aim of this book was to point out all the planning and communication work one must do upfront in order to have a smooth roll-out of a global system and avoid the problems of our VP. There are two central messages we hope you take away from the book. First, there is a lot of work that must be done "before the train leaves the station" in global selection. Second, the rewards of that work, an effective, global selection process, are rich. Once you have finished collecting and integrating input, sorting through cultural and linguistic and labor market and legal issues, and ensuring system effectiveness, the results will be well-worth your effort.

In this last chapter, we'd like to prognosticate upcoming trends and challenges that will make global staffing systems increasingly important, more likely to be adopted, and easier to implement.

Trends and Challenges

• Growth in global business and industry

There is no doubt that there is an obvious trend toward the expansion of business and industry beyond home countries. We expect there to be continued demand for international workers who can function effectively anywhere on the globe and for selection systems to identify these workers. We also anticipate continued pressure for staffing efficiencies that will make global selection systems mandatory. Competitive organizations can no longer afford redundant staffing and selection systems.

• Increasing convergence in HR practices

In Chapter 1 we noted that there are different views on the extent to which cultures are converging on a global basis. However, it is clear that with greater and greater connectivity comes greater convergence. With exposure to best practices from around the globe, organizations will adopt the best HR practices that maximize transportability and effectiveness. Hence, we expect that the next decade will lead to even greater convergence in how selection is done on a global basis.

• Enhanced skills in managing cross-cultural efforts

In our view, the rapid growth in the field of international human resources, including growth in course offerings and specialty MBA programs, academic research to support the undertaking of global HR systems, and in the number of managers who possess experience and skill in working in different cultures and/or working with culturally diverse teams all bode well for the future ability of companies to implement global staffing systems.

• Shrinking technology gaps

While we emphasize throughout the book that you need to be aware of differences in technological resources in different locations, it is clear that access to technology continue to improve. The narrowing technology gaps can only make global staffing systems easier to implement and monitor. For example, while only eight countries had Internet access in 1988, over 200 had access in 2000, and ever since the number of users has grown exponentially (4).

• Increasing convergence in legal environments

We noted in Chapter 4 that the European Union has made strides toward convergence in employment discrimination law within Europe.

Although certainly there remain many differences across countries in terms of laws and in the rights of workers (and job applicants), we do see continued steps toward greater similarities. This may be a long process with no complete convergence in sight, but international agreement on what constitutes acceptable employee selection is growing.

While there are some environmental aspects that will make global staffing easier to support and implement, there are also trends that will continue to make undertaking a global selection system a challenge. Here's what we think will remain a challenge for global staffing:

• Disparities in skill levels and education across countries

In the USA, there is a great deal of concern over the gap between the skill requirements of new jobs and the current skill level of many individuals in the workforce. At a global level, there are clear disparities across countries in skills needed for today's jobs. One in every five adults worldwide is functionally illiterate – although this is a substantial improvement over the situation in 1970, when one in three was illiterate (1), this lack of education in some regions of the globe will be a continuing challenge for those seeking to hire skilled workers who possess the abilities to learn quickly and acquire new skills as their work changes in a global economy.

• Disparities in economic environments across countries

While there are many emerging markets that have experienced significant levels of economic growth, there are many regions that remain burdened with extraordinarily high poverty rates. For example, nearly 70 percent of the African workforce is concentrated in agriculture, with unemployment rates in countries often above 20 or 30 percent (2). Nearly half of the population in Africa lives on less than $1 a day (2). While there are many individuals engaged in efforts to change the economic state of some countries, it would be naïve to view disparities in economic environments as something that will be quickly eradicated. It would also be foolish to ignore the implications of struggling economies for your selection system.

• Lack of off-the-shelf, well-developed, well-translated, and validated tools ready for global implementation

While there are numerous vendors of selection tools, most do not currently have off-the-shelf products that have been validated in multiple countries that can be implemented quickly. The past ten years or so have seen an increase in well-translated versions of existing tools, but much still needs to be done to gather the validity evidence and equivalence evidence we have talked about in this book. Organizations seeking to go global with their staffing processes are still likely to need to budget time and money for development, translation, and the evaluation of selection procedures.

• Competition for talent in expanding markets

Our points regarding skills gaps and education gaps relate to the difficulties of recruiting in expanding markets. A recent report on future human capital challenges (3) notes that one of the key issues for organizations, both large and small, is the competition for talented employees. As more organizations hire globally rather than locally, the pool of potential applicants for jobs expands, but so does the competition for those individuals willing to work abroad.

• High coordination costs

In numerous places throughout this book we've noted that you need to plan and budget for various issues associated with implementation of a system, not just its development. There are also some expenses associated with working globally that one must recognize will add to every step of the process of designing a new system. These include (4):

• Communication costs. Costs of communicating with a remote team (telephone, fax, express mail).
• Overtime costs. Possibly paying for work time outside of normal hours for some team members (depending on team methods of communication as well as wage structures and the specific positions of team members).
• Travel costs. Some travel necessary for effective coordination of this type of project.

In closing, we would like to emphasize that developing a global staffing system is not a quick and easy matter of simply taking something working in one place and using it in another. The process requires many different types of expertise – internal experts on local cultures and history, experts on legal environments, experts in test development and validation, translators, internal experts on the organization's strategic direction and goals, and so on. Although the challenges of developing and implementing global selection systems remain formidable, we hope this book has provided you with the questions to ask of these various experts that will enable you to make good choices as you embark on a global selection system.

References for Chapter 7

1 World Resources Institute, 2008.
2 http://t21.ca/employ/index.htm; 2008.
3 SHRM Foundation, 2007.
4 Testa, 2008.

References

Books and Journals

American Educational Research Association, American Psychological Association, & National Council on Measurement in Education. (1999). *Standards for educational and psychological testing.* Washington, DC: American Educational Research Association.

Anderson, N., & Witvliet, C. (2008). Fairness reactions to personnel selection methods: An international comparison between the Netherlands, the United States, France, Spain, Portugal, and Singapore. *International Journal of Selection and Assessment, 16,* 1–13.

Ashkanasy, N., Gupta, V., Mayfield, M. S., & Trevor-Roberts, E. (2004). Future orientation. In R. J. House, P. J. Hanges, M. Javidan, P. W. Dorfman, & V. Gupta (Eds.), *Culture, leadership, and organizations: The GLOBE study of 62 societies* (pp. 282–342). Thousand Oaks, CA: Sage.

Avery, D. R., Hernandez, M., & Hebl, M. R. (2004). Who's watching the race? Racial salience in recruitment advertising. *Journal of Applied Social Psychology, 34*(1), 146–61.

Baack, D. W., & Singh, N. (2007). Culture and web communications. *Journal of Business Research, 60,* 181–8.

Bartram, D. (2007, April). *Global norms? Some guidelines for aggregating personality norms across countries.* Presented at the 22nd annual meeting of the Society for Industrial and Organizational Psychology, New York.

Beller, M., Gafni, N., & Hanani, P. (2005). Constructing, adapting, and validating admissions tests in multiple languages: The Israeli case. In R. K. Hambleton, P. F. Merenda, & C. D. Spielberger (Eds.), *Adapting educational and psychological tests for cross-cultural assessment* (pp. 297–320). Mahwah, NJ: Lawrence Erlbaum.

171

Bertolino, M., & Steiner D. D. (2007). Fairness reactions to selection methods: An Italian study. *International Journal of Selection and Assessment, 15,* 197–205.

Bhagat, R. S., Van Scotter, J. R., Steverson, P. K., & Moustafa, K (2007). Cultural variations in individual job performance: Implications for industrial and organizational psychology in the 21st century. *International Review of Industrial and Organizational Psychology, 22,* 235–64.

Bhasin B. B. (2007). Succeeding in China: Cultural adjustments for Indian businesses. *Cross-Cultural Management: An International Journal, 14,* 43–53.

Bhaskaran, S., & Sukumaran, N. (2007). National culture, business culture and management practices: Consequential relationships? *Cross-Cultural Management: An International Journal, 14,* 54–67.

Bjorkman, I., & Lervik, J. E. (2007). Transferring HR practices within multinational corporations. *Human Resource Management Journal, 17,* 320–35.

Blum-Kulka, S., Danet, D., & Gherson, R. (1985). The language of requesting in Israeli society. In J. Forgas (Ed.), *Language and social situations* (pp. 113–39). New York: Springer.

Bontempo, R. (1993). Translation fidelity of psychological scales: An item response theory analysis of an individualism-collectivism scale. *Journal of Cross-Cultural Psychology, 24*(2), 149–66.

Borstorff, P. C., Harris, S. G., Field, H. S., & Giles, W. F. (1997). Who'll go? A review of factors associated with employee willingness to work overseas. *Human Resource Planning, 20,* 29–40.

Brandel, M. (2006, November 20). Fishing in the Global talent pool. *Computerworld, 40*(47), 33–5.

Brannick, M. T. & Levine, E. L. (2002). *Job analysis: Methods, research and applications for human resource management in the new millennium.* Thousand Oaks, CA: Sage.

Breaugh, J., & Starke, M. (2000). Research on employee recruiting: So many studies, so many remaining questions. *Journal of Management, 26,* 405–34.

Brewster, C. (2006). Comparing HRM policies and practices across geographical borders. In G. K. Stahl & I. Bjorkman (Eds.), *Handbook of research in international human resource management* (pp. 68–90). Cheltenham, UK: Edward Elgar.

Briscoe, D. (1997). Assessment centers: Cross-cultural and cross-national issues. *Journal of Social Behavior and Personality, 12,* 261–70.

Brislin, R., Worthley, R., & MacNab, B. (2006) Cultural intelligence: Understanding behaviors that serve people's goals. *Group & Organization Management, 31,* 40–55.

Brislin, R. W. (1986). The wording and translation of research instruments. In W. J. Lonner & J. W. Berry (Eds.), *Field methods in cross-cultural research* (pp. 137–64). Newbury Park, CA: Sage.

Burns, S. R., Davis, S. F., Hoshino, J., & Miller, R. L. (1998). Academic dishonesty: A delineation of cross-cultural patterns. *College Student Journal, 32*(4), 590–6.

Carl, D., Gupta, V., & Javidan, M. (2004). Power distance. In R. J. House, P. J. Hanges, M. Javidan, P. W. Dorfman, & V. Gupta (Eds.), *Culture, leadership, and organizations: The GLOBE study of 62 societies* (pp. 513–63). Thousand Oaks, CA: Sage.

Chao, G. T., & Nguyen, H. D. (2005). International employment discrimination: A review of legal issues, human impacts, and organizational implications. In R. L. Dipboye & A. Colella (Eds.), *Discrimination at work: The psychological and organizational bases* (pp. 379–408). Mahwah, NJ: Lawrence Erlbaum.

Church, A. T., Katigbak, M. S., del Prado, A. M., Valdez-Medina, J. L., Miramontes, L. G., & Ortiz, F. A. (2006). A cross-cultural study of trait self-enhancement, explanatory variables and adjustment. *Journal of Research in Personality, 40,* 1169–201.

Collings, D. G., & Scullion, H. (2006a). Approaches to international staffing. In H. Scullion & D.G. Collings (Eds.), *Global staffing* (pp. 17–38). London: Routledge.

Collings, D. G., & Scullion, H. (2006b). Global staffing. In G. K. Stahl & I. Bjorkman (Eds.), *Handbook of research in international human resource management* (pp. 141–57). Cheltenham, UK: Edward Elgar.

Collings, D. G., Scullion, H., & Morley, M. J. (2007). Changing patterns of global staffing in the multinational enterprise: Challenges to the conventional expatriate assignment and emerging alternatives. *Journal of World Business, 42,* 198–213.

Colvin, G. (2007, December 10). The battle for brainpower. *Fortune,* 24–6.

Cullen, L. T. (2007, October 22). The new expatriates. *Time: Global supplement section,* 1–4.

Cunningham, L. X., & Rowley, C. (2007). Human resource management in Chinese small and medium enterprises. *Personnel Review, 36,* 415–39.

Davis, S. L., & Finney, S. J. (2006). A factor analytic study of the cross-cultural adaptability inventory. *Educational and Psychological Measurement, 66,* 318–30.

Diamantopoulos, A., Reynolds, N. L., & Simintiras, A. C. (2006). The impact of response styles on the stability of cross-national comparisons. *Journal of Business Research, 59,* 925–35.

Donthu, N., & Yoo, B. (1998). Cultural influences on service quality expectations. *Journal of Service Research, 1,* 178–86.

Duignan, R., & Yoshida, K. (2007). Employee perceptions of recent work environment changes in Japan. *Personnel Review, 36,* 440–56.

Earley, P. C., & Ang, S. (2003). *Cultural intelligence: Individual interactions across cultures.* Palo Alto, CA: Stanford University Press.

Edstrum, A., & Galbraith, J. R. (1977). Transfer of managers as a coordination and control strategy in multinational organizations. *Administrative Science Quarterly, 22,* 248–64.

Edwards, T., Colling, T. R., & Ferner, A. (2007). Conceptual approaches to the transfer of employment practices in multinational companies: An integrated approach. *Human Resource Management Journal, 17,* 201–17.

Eggebeen, S. (2002). Going global: Additional considerations inherent in cross-cultural implementation. In J. W. Hedge & E. D. Pulakos (Eds.), *Implementing organizational interventions* (pp. 270–96). San Francisco: Jossey-Bass.

European Commission. (2007). Discrimination in the European Union. Published by the European Commission. Online at http://ec.europa.eu/public_opinion/archives/ebs/ebs_263_sum_en.pdf.

Farndale, E., & Paauwe, J. (2007). Uncovering competitive and institutional drivers of HRM practices in multinational corporations. *Human Resource Management Journal, 17,* 355–75.

Fields, D., Chan, A., Akhtar, S., & Blum, T. C. (2006). Human resource management strategies under uncertainty: How do U.S. and Hong Kong Chinese companies differ? *Cross-Cultural Management: An International Journal, 13,* 171–86.

Fischer, R. (2006). Congruence and functions of personal and cultural values: Do my values reflect my culture's values? *Personality and Social Psychology Bulletin, 32,* 1419–31.

Frisby, C. L. (1999). Culture and test session behavior: Part II. *School Psychology Quarterly, 14,* 281–303.

Garcia, M. F., Posthuma, R. A., & Roehling, M. V. (2008, April). *How does national culture predict preference for employing males or local nationals?* Presented at the Annual Conference of the Society for Industrial and Organizational Psychology, San Francisco.

Gelfand, M. J., Bhawuk, D. P. S., Nishii, L. H., & Bechtold, D. J. (2004). Individualism and collectivism. In R. J. House, P. J. Hanges, M. Javidan, P. W. Dorfman, & V. Gupta (Eds.), *Culture, leadership, and organizations: The GLOBE study of 62 societies* (pp. 437–512). Thousand Oaks, CA: Sage.

Gelfand, M. J., Nishii, L. H., & Raver, J. L. (2006). On the nature and importance of cultural tightness-looseness. *Journal of Applied Psychology, 91,* 1225–44.

Gerhart, B., & Fang, M. (2005). National culture and human resource management: Assumptions and evidence. *International Journal of Human Resource Management, 16*, 971–86.

Gilliland, S. W., & Cherry, B. (2000). Managing "customers" of selection processes. In J. F. Kehoe (Ed.), *Managing selection in changing organizations* (pp. 158–96). San Francisco: Jossey-Bass.

Grimm, S. D., & Church, A. T. (1999). A cross-cultural study of response biases in personality measures. *Journal of Research in Personality, 33*, 415–41.

Groeschl, S. (2003). Cultural implications for the appraisal process. *Cross-Cultural Management, 10*, 67–79.

Groh, K., & Allen, M. (1998). Global staffing: Are expatriates the only answer? *HR Focus, 75*, S1.

Guion, R. M. (1998). *Assessment, measurement, and prediction for personnel decisions.* Mahwah, NJ: Lawrence Erlbaum.

Hambleton, R. K. (2005). Issues, designs, and technical guidelines for adapting tests into multiple languages and cultures. In R. K. Hambleton, P. F. Merenda, & C. D. Spielberger (Eds.), *Adapting educational and psychological tests for cross-cultural assessment* (pp. 3–38). Mahwah, NJ: Lawrence Erlbaum.

Hansen, F. (2006). Paperless route for recruiting. *Workforce Management, 85*, 34–7.

Hansen, F. (2008). Microsoft's Canadian move a swipe at stiff U.S. visa policies. *Workforce Management,* online, http://www.workforce.com/section/06/feature/25/33/66. Downloaded on February 14, 2008.

Harvey, M. G., Novicevic, M. M., & Speier, C. (2000). Strategic global human resource management: The role of inpatriate managers. *Human Resource Management Review, 10*, 153–75.

Hazucha, J., Ramesh, A., Bank, J., & Sevy, B. (2007, April). *Global norms and organizational decisions.* Presented at the annual meetings of the Society for Industrial and Organizational Psychology, New York.

Higgs. A. C., Papper, E. M., & Carr, I. S. (2000). Integrating selection with other organizational processes and systems. In J. F. Kehoe (Ed.), *Managing selection in changing organizations* (pp. 73–122). San Francisco: Jossey-Bass.

Hofstede, G. (1980). *Culture's consequences: International differences in work-related values.* London: Sage.

House, R., Hanges, P., Javidan, M., Dorfman, P., & Gupta, V. (Eds.). (2004). *Culture, leadership, and organizations: The GLOBE study of 62 societies.* Thousand Oaks, CA: Sage.

House, R., Javidan, M., Hanges, P., & Dorfman, P. (2002). Understanding cultures and implicit leadership theories across the globe: An introduction to project GLOBE. *Journal of World Business, 37*(1), 3–10.

Howard, A., Erker, S., & Bruce, N. (2007). *Selection forecast 2006/2007: Slugging through the war for talent.* Pittsburgh, PA: Development Dimensions International.

Hui, C. H., & Triandis, H. C. (1989). Effects of culture and response format on extreme response style. *Journal of Cross-Cultural Psychology, 20,* 296–309.

Huo, Y. P., Huang, H. J., & Napier, N. K. (2002). Divergence or convergence: A cross-national comparison of personnel selection practices. *Human Resource Management, 41,* 31–44.

International Test Commission. (2001). *International Test Commission guidelines for test adaptation.* London: Author.

Ivener, M. (2006). Stopped at the border. *HR Magazine, 51,* 116–20.

Javidan, M., & House, R. J. (2001). Cultural acumen for the global manager: Lessons from project GLOBE. *Organizational Dynamics, 29,* 289–305.

Kaminski, K. A., & Hemingway, M. A. (2008, April). *Assessment around the world: A case study from Starwood Hotels.* Presented at Annual Conference of the Society for Industrial and Organizational Psychology, San Francisco.

Katriel, T. (1986). *Talking straight: Dugri Speech in Israeli Sabra Culture.* Cambridge: Cambridge University Press.

Kostova, T., & Roth, K (2002). Adoption of an organizational practice by subsidiaries of multinational corporations: Institutional and relational effects. *Academy of Management Journal, 45,* 215–33.

Leventhal, G. (1980). What should be done with equity theory? New approaches to the study of fairness in social relationships. In K. J. Gergen, M. S. Greenberg, & R. H. Willis (Eds.), *Social exchanges: Advances in theory and research* (pp. 27–55). New York: Plenum Press.

Lim, C., Winter, R., & Chan, C. C. A. (2006). Cross-cultural interviewing in the hiring process: Challenges and strategies. *The Career Development Quarterly, 54,* 265–8.

Lupton, R. A., & Chapman, K. J. (2002). Russian and American college students' attitudes, perceptions and tendencies towards cheating. *Educational Research, 44*(1), 17–27.

Marcus, B. (2003). Attitudes towards personnel selection methods: A partial replication and extension in a German sample. *Applied Psychology: An International Review, 52,* 515–32.

McDaniel, M. A., Morgeson, F. P., Finnegan, E. B., Campion, M. A., & Braverman, E. P. (2001). Use of situational judgment tests to predict job performance: A clarification of the literature. *Journal of Applied Psychology, 86*(4), 730–40.

McKay, C. (2007). 9 tips for increasing translation quality while decreasing translation cost. Downloaded from www.translationdirectory.com/article413.htm on December 11.

McNerney, D. J. (1996). Global staffing: Some common problems – and solutions. *HR Focus, 73*, 1–4.

Moscoso, S., & Salgado, J. R. (2004). Fairness reactions to personnel selection techniques in Spain and Portugal. *International Journal of Selection and Assessment, 12*, 187–96.

Myloni, B., Harzing, A., & Mirza, H. (2007). Human resource management in Greece: Have the colours of culture faded away? *International Journal of Cross-Cultural Management, 4*, 59–76.

Myors, B., Lievens, F., Schollaert, E., Van Hoye, G., Cronshaw, S. F., et al. (2008). International perspectives on the legal environment for selection. *Industrial and Organizational Psychology: Perspectives on Science and Practice, 1*, 206–46.

Ng, K., & Earley, P. C. (2006). Culture + intelligence: Old constructs, new frontiers. *Group & Organization Management, 31*, 4–19.

Nikolaou, I., & Judge T. A. (2007). Fairness reactions to personnel selection techniques in Greece: The role of core self-evaluations. *International Journal of Selection and Assessment, 15*, 206–19.

Nisbett, R. E. (2003). *The geography of thought: How Asians and Westerners think differently . . . and why*. New York: The Free Press.

Nyfield, G., & Baron, H. (2000). Cultural context in adapting selection practices across borders. In J. Kehoe (Ed.), *Managing selection in changing organizations: Human resource strategies* (pp. 242–70). San Francisco: Jossey-Bass.

Odendaal, A., de Bruin, G. P., & Roodt, G. (2007, April). *Cross-cultural differences in social desirability scores in South Africa*. Presented at the annual meeting of the Society for Industrial and Organizational Psychology, New York.

Oyserman, D., Coon, H. M., & Kemmelmeier, M. (2002). Rethinking individualism and collectivism: Evaluation of theoretical assumptions and meta-analyses. *Psychological Bulletin, 128*, 3–72.

Papalexandris, N., & Panayotopoulou, L. (2004). Exploring the mutual interaction of societal culture and human resource management practices: Evidence from 19 countries. *Employee Relations, 26*, 495–509.

Peppas, S. C., & Yu, T. (2005). Job candidate attributes: A comparison of Chinese and US employer evaluations and the perceptions of Chinese students. *Cross-Cultural Management, 12*, 78–91.

Perkins, L. A., Thomas, K. M., & Taylor, G. A. (2000). Advertising and recruitment: Marketing to minorities. *Psychology & Marketing, 17*, 235–55.

Phillips, J. M., & Gully, S. M. (2002). Fairness reactions to personnel selection techniques in Singapore and the United States. *International Journal of Human Resource Management, 13*, 1186–205.

Pires, G., Stanton, J., & Ostenfeld, S. (2006). Improving expatriate adjustment and effectiveness in ethnically diverse countries: Marketing insights. *Cross-Cultural Management: An International Journal, 13*, 156–70.

Ployhart, R. E., Wiechmann, D., Schmitt, N., Sacco, J. M., & Rogg, K. (2003). The cross-cultural equivalence of job performance ratings. *Human Performance, 16*, 49–79.

Posthuma, R. A., Roehling, M. V., & Campion, M. A. (2006). Applying US employment discrimination laws to international employers: Advice for scientists and practitioners. *Personnel Psychology, 59*, 705–40.

Pratt, A. K., Biga, A., Gibby, R. E., & Irwin, J. L. (2008, April). *Cultural influences on global biographical data instruments.* Presented at the Annual Conference of the Society for Industrial and Organizational Psychology, San Francisco.

Rosenzweig, P. M. (2006). The dual logics behind international human resource management: Pressures for global integration and local responsiveness. In G. K. Stahl & I. Bjorkman (Eds.), *Handbook of research in international human resource management* (pp. 36–48). Cheltenham, UK: Edward Elgar.

Rothstein-Fisch, C., Trumbull, E., Isaac, A., Daley, C., & Perez, A. I. (2003). When "helping someone else" is the right answer: Bridging cultures in assessment. *Journal of Latinos and Education, 2*(3), 123–40.

Ryan, A. M., Boyce, A. S., Ghumman, S., Jundt, D., Schmidt, G., & Gibby, R. (in press). Going global: Cultural values and perceptions of selection procedures. *Applied Psychology: An International Review.*

Ryan, A. M., & Delany, T. (in press). Attraction to organizations. In N. T. Tippins & J. Farr (Eds.), *Handbook of employee selection.* Blackwell.

Ryan, A. M., Hemingway, M., Carr, J., & Highhouse, S. (unpublished manuscript). *Stakeholder needs and selection system criteria.* East Lansing: Michigan State University, Department of Psychology.

Ryan, A. M., McFarland, L., Baron, H., & Page, R. C. (1999). An international look at selection practices: Nation and culture as explanations for variability in practice. *Personnel Psychology, 52*, 359–92.

Ryan, A. M., & Tippins, N. T. (2003). Attracting and selecting: What psychological research tells us. *Human Resource Management, 43*(4), 305–18.

Ryan, A. M., Wiechmann, D., & Hemingway, M. (2003). Designing and implementing global staffing systems: Part II – best practices. *Human Resource Management, 42*, 85–94.

Schmidt, F. L., & Hunter, J. E. (1998). The validity and utility of selection methods in personnel psychology: Practical and theoretical implications of 85 years of research findings. *Psychological Bulletin, 124*, 262–74.

Schmitt, D. P., Allik, J., McCrae, R. R., & Benet-Martinez, V. (2007). The geographic distribution of Big Five personality traits: Patterns and profiles of human self-description across 56 nations. *Journal of Cross-Cultural Psychology, 38*(2), 173–212.

Schuler, R. S., & Tarique, I. (2007). International human resource management: A thematic update and suggestions for future research. *International Journal of Human Resource Management, 18*, 717–44.

Schwartz, S. H., & Boehnke, K. (2004). Evaluating the structure of human values with confirmatory factor analysis. *Journal of Research in Personality, 38*(3), 230–55.

Segalla, M., Sauquet, A., & Turati, C. (2001). Symbolic vs. functional recruitment: Cultural influences on employee recruitment policy. *European Management Journal, 19*, 32–43.

Shimoni, B., & Bergmann, H. (2007). Managing in a changing world: From multiculturalism to hybridization – the production of hybrid management cultures in Israel, Thailand, and Mexico. *Academy of Management Perspectives, 20*, 76–89.

Shin, S. J., Morgeson, F. P., & Campion, M. A. (2007). What you do depends on where you are: Understanding how domestic and expatriate work requirements depend upon the cultural context. *Journal of International Business Studies, 38*, 64–83.

Smith, P. B. (2004). Acquiescent response bias as an aspect of cultural communication style. *Journal of Cross-Cultural Psychology, 35*, 50–61.

Smith, P. B., Dugan, S., & Trompenaars, F. (1996). National culture and the values of organizational employees: A dimensional analysis across 43 nations. *Journal of Cross-Cultural Psychology, 27*(2), 231–64.

Society for Industrial and Organizational Psychology. (2003). *Principles for the validation and use of personnel selection procedures.* San Francisco: Jossey-Bass.

Society for Human Resource Management Foundation. (2007, December). *Strategic research on human capital challenges.* SHRM Foundation.

Solomon, C. M. (1996). Big Mac's McGlobal HR secrets. *Personnel Journal, 75*, 46–51.

Spielberger, C. D., Moscoso, M. S., & Brunner, T. M. (2005). Cross-cultural assessment of emotional states and personality traits. In R. K. Hambleton, P. F. Merenda, & C. D. Spielberger (Eds.), *Adapting educational and psychological tests for cross-cultural assessment* (pp. 343–68). Mahwah, NJ: Lawrence Erlbaum.

Steiner, D. D., & Gilliland, S. W. (1996). Fairness reactions to personnel selection techniques in France and the United States. *Journal of Applied Psychology, 81*, 134–41.

Steiner, D. D., & Gilliland, S. W. (2001). Procedural justice in personnel selection: International and cross-cultural perspectives. *International Journal of Selection and Assessment, 9*, 124–37.

Stone, D. L., Stone-Romero, E. F., & Lukaszewski, K. M. (2007). The impact of cultural values on the acceptance and effectiveness of human resource management policies and practices. *Human Resource Management Review, 17*, 152–65.

Sue-Chan, C., & Dasborough, M. T. (2006). The influence of relation-based and rule-based regulations on hiring decisions in the Australian and Hong Kong Chinese cultural contexts. *International Journal of Human Resource Management, 17*, 1267–92.

Sully de Luque, M., & Javidan, M. (2004). Uncertainty avoidance. In R. J. House, P. J. Hanges, M. Javidan, P. W. Dorfman, & V. Gupta (Eds.), *Culture, leadership, and organizations: The GLOBE study of 62 societies* (pp. 602–53). Thousand Oaks, CA: Sage.

Tan, D., & Mahoney, J. T. (2006). Why a multinational firm chooses expatriates: Integrating resource-based, agency and transaction costs perspectives. *Journal of Management Studies, 42*, 457–84.

Taylor, P. J., Li, W., Shi, K., & Borman, W. C. (2008). The transportability of job information across countries. *Personnel Psychology, 61*(1), 69–111.

Testa, B. M. (2008). Coordination costs of offshoring. *Workforce Management*. Downloaded from www.workforce.com on 2/29/08.

The Wharton School. (2008). Made in China. *Human Resource Executive Online*. Downloaded from www.hreonline.com on 2/25/08.

Thomas, D. C. (2006). Domain and development of cultural intelligence: The importance of mindfulness. *Group & Organization Management, 31*, 78–99.

Tippins, N. T. (2002). Issues in implementing large-scale selection programs: In J. W. Hedge & E. D. Pulakos (Eds.), *Implementing organization interventions: Steps, processes, and best practices* (pp. 232–69). San Francisco: Jossey-Bass.

Triandis, H. C. (2006). Cultural intelligence in organizations. *Group & Organization Management, 31*, 20–6.

Tsui, A. S., Nifadkar, S. S., & Ou, A. Y. (2007). Cross-national, cross-cultural organizational behavior research: Advances, gaps and recommendations. *Journal of Management, 33*, 426–78.

Tye, M., & Snider-Lotz, T. (2007). Feasibility of assessing in non-native languages to predict job performance. Presented at the annual meeting of the Society for Industrial and Organizational Psychology, New York.

Uday-Riley, M. (2006). Eight critical steps to improve workplace performance with cross-cultural teams. *Performance Improvement, 45*, 28–32.

Vance, C. M., & Paik, Y. (2006). *Managing a global workforce: Challenges and opportunities in International Human Resource Management*. London, England: M. E. Sharpe.

Van de Vijver, F. J. R., & Poortinga, Y. H. (2005). Conceptual and methodological issues in adapting tests. In R. K. Hambleton, P. F. Merenda, & C. D. Spielberger (Eds.), *Adapting educational and psychological tests for cross-cultural assessment* (pp. 39–64). Mahwah, NJ: Lawrence Erlbaum.

Varela, O., Esqueda, S., & Perez, O. (2008, April). *A test of cross-culture homogeneity in Latin America: A structural equation modeling application.* Presented at the Annual Conference of the Society for Industrial and Organizational Psychology, San Francisco.

Wan, C., Chiu, C., Tam, K., Lee, S., Lau, I. Y., & Peng, S. (2007). Perceived cultural importance and actual self-importance of values in cultural identification. *Journal of Personality and Social Psychology, 92,* 337–54.

Wiechmann, D., Ryan, A. M., & Hemingway, M. (2003). Designing and implementing global staffing systems: Part I – leaders in global staffing. *Human Resource Management, 42,* 71–83.

World Bank. (2007, Sept. 26). *Doing business in 2008 (178 economics – comparing regulations).* Washington, DC: World Bank.

World Resources Institute. (2008). *Communications and tomorrow's markets.* Downloaded from www.writ.org on 2/8/08.

Yasin, M. M., & Yavas, U. (2007). An analysis of E-business practices in the Arab culture. *Cross-Cultural Management: An International Journal, 14,* 68–73.

Websites

http://www.wachovia.com/inside/page/0,,137_371_372_374,00.html. Downloaded 2/27/08.

http://www.personal.barclays.co.uk/BRC1/jsp/brccontrol?task=articleFWab out&site=pfs&value=13465&menu=5500. Downloaded 2/27/08.

http://www.bmwusfactory.com/build/. Downloaded 2/27/08.

http://www.isp.state.id.us/hr/trooper_info/realistic_job.html. Downloaded 2/27/08.

http://www.brucepower.com/uc/GetDocument.aspx?docid=2288. Downloaded 2/27/08.

http://www.dungarvin.com/Employment/Realistic%20Job%20Preview/ RJP-page01.html. Downloaded 2/27/08.

http://t21.ca/employ/index.htm. Downloaded 2/8/08.

Index

3M, 18, 115

acceptability considerations, in tool
  choice, 42, 133–4
acquiescence, 81, 131–2
adaptation
  ITC Guidelines, 130–1
  of tools for global use, 124–33;
    administration aids, 133;
    evidence of equivalence,
    131–2; instructions, 133
  see also translation
administration
  considerations in tool choice,
    41–2
  consistency, 18
  online platforms, 134–5
  and selection system
    effectiveness, 57,
    152–4
administrators
  selection, 136–7
  training, 136–7, 153
Africa, poverty, 167
Agilent Technologies, 1, 16
analytic thinking, 77

applicants
  expectations, 34, 38, 155; cultural
    differences and, 78–9
  fairness perceptions, 59
  orientation materials, 59, 156
  selection of best, 27–8
  source, 10
  technological capacities, 19
application forms, use by country,
  66–7
Arabic, translation to, 128
Argentina, hierarchical values,
  82
assertiveness, 76
assessment, accuracy vs. cost, 28–9
assessment centers
  costs, 52
  definition, 31
  validity, 52
Association of South East Asian
    Nations (ASEAN) Free Trade
    Area, 104
assumptions, of selection systems,
  25–9
attraction, of candidates, 159
audits, 158